OXFORD MEDICAL PUBLICATIONS

Health for All Children

D0784832

Health for All Children

A Programme for Child Health Surveillance

The Report of the Joint Working Party
on Child Health Surveillance

Edited by

DAVID M. B. HALL

*Consultant and Honorary Senior Lecturer
in Community Child Health,
St George's Hospital Medical School, London*

OXFORD   NEW YORK   TOKYO
OXFORD UNIVERSITY PRESS

Oxford University Press, Walton Street, Oxford OX2 6DP

Oxford New York Toronto
Delhi Bombay Calcutta Madras Karachi
Petaling Jaya Singapore Hong Kong Tokyo
Nairobi Dar es Salaam Cape Town
Melbourne Auckland

and associated companies in
Berlin Ibadan

Oxford is a trade mark of Oxford University Press

Published in the United States
by Oxford University Press, New York

First published 1989
Reprinted 1989

British Library Cataloguing in Publication Data

Joint Working Party on Child Health
Surveillance.
Health for all children : report of a
Joint Working Party on Child Health
Surveillance.
1. Children. Health. Assessment
I. Title   II. Hall, David M.B.
613.'0432

ISBN 0-19-261815-6

Library of Congress Cataloging in Publication Data

Joint Working Party on Child Health Surveillance (Great Britain)
Health for all children : report of a Joint Working Party on Child
Health Surveillance / edited by David M.B. Hall.
Bibliography
1. Children—Diseases—Diagnosis.   2. Child health services.
I. Hall, David M.B.   II. Title.
RJ50.J65   1989   362.1'9892—dc19   88-39388

ISBN 0-19-261815-6

Printed and bound in Great Britain by
Biddles Ltd, Guildford and King's Lynn

Foreword

by

Kenneth Clark
Secretary of State for Health

and

Malcolm Rifkind
Secretary of State for Scotland

The prevention of ill health and the promotion of good health are key features of the Government's health policy. Effective child health services, which seek to improve the health of young people at formative stages, play an important role in improving the nation's health for the future. We welcome the initiative of the relevant professional bodies in forming the Joint Working Party on Child Health Surveillance, whose remit was to examine existing services and to make recommendations for future practice. Improvements in the service can only come about through a multi-disciplinary consideration of the issues involved and the working party is to be congratulated on the balanced report it has produced. This report clearly points the way forward and we feel sure that it will be welcomed by all those who are keen to provide a coherent and effective programme of health surveillance throughout the childhood years.

We are particularly pleased to see the emphasis in the report on the role of parents and on health education. These two elements have been neglected in the past and it is most encouraging to see that their rightful role in child health services is fully recognized.

Preface

Child health surveillance is concerned with the prevention of disease, the early detection of problems affecting growth and development, and the positive promotion of health. These are laudable goals but they must be precisely defined. Benevolent intentions are not enough.

In the past few years, there has been increasing interest in the role and value of routine child health surveillance. The lack of consensus on these issues was recognized and informal discussions were arranged between the British Paediatric Association and the Royal College of General Practitioners, the General Medical Services Committee of the British Medical Association, the Health Visitors' Association, and the Royal College of Nursing. In January 1986 a working party was established with representatives from each of these organizations. Observers were also invited from the World Health Organization, the Department of Health and Social Security, and the Scottish Home and Health Department.

The working party was given the following terms of reference:

'To review and comment upon current practice in child health surveillance in the United Kingdom and to make recommendations for future practice.'

This report is the result of two years' work by the joint working party. It offers a critical analysis of the many aspects of professional activity collectively known as child health surveillance. Many of us began with preconceived ideas on the subject, but as a result of many debates between ourselves and with specialists in various fields, and through a detailed study of the literature, we have been persuaded to modify our views.

In preparing this report, we have been able to draw on an immense body of knowledge and experience accumulated by doctors, psychologists, therapists, and education specialists over the past 20 years. The interest in child development and handicap, which was stimulated by the work of the pioneers in this field, has resulted in a substantial improvement in the care available to children in this country.

It now seems appropriate to review what has been learned and to consider how this new knowledge and insight can be incorporated into child surveillance. In suggesting changes to the pattern of clinical practice, we are not implying that all the activity of the last 20 years has been wasted. On the contrary, the experience gained has provided the essential foundation from which the subject can be developed.

The programme recommended in our report may well cause anxiety to many doctors, nurses, and managers, at least in some parts of Britain, because it implies a reduction in the number of screening tests and procedures. We recognize and respect their concerns, but wish to emphasize that we have rejected only those activities for which no scientific justification can be found. Furthermore, we have placed a greater emphasis than previous workers on the role of parents in detecting disorders in their children and in sharing their care. On the other hand, we have laid great stress on the quality of care. The importance of early diagnosis of disabling childhood conditions has been highlighted, not because they are necessarily curable, but because this is what parents want.

Although community child health involves the delivery of certain aspects of health care to the whole population rather than responding to individual anxieties about illness, the maintenance of high clinical standards is no less important. The quality of the work done in each clinical transaction must always be considered, as well as the numbers of contacts or tests performed. We have suggested some ways in which quality can be monitored and assured. This approach has far-reaching implications for other aspects of health care.

Furthermore, we have argued that the detection of defects is only one of the goals of surveillance and that health promotion deserves much greater commitment. For example, high uptake of immunization and programmes of accident prevention can be achieved only if adequate professional time is available. Clinicians and managers will need to consider how these goals can be pursued, while at the same time ensuring that staff retain the flexibility and freedom to provide appropriate care for the individual child and family. The programme we recommend is not merely a collection of tests, but a global approach to child health. We urge all who have responsibility for child health services to read the report in its entirety!

We have deliberately avoided the question of which professionals should carry out the various tasks we have specified. It will be clear from our report that we consider the acquisition of appropriate knowledge, attitudes, and skills, and the formation of a constructive relationship with the family, to be more important than the individual's original professional background.

The costs of implementing our recommendations will vary considerably according to local conditions. It is always more difficult to deliver a programme of health care in areas of urban or rural deprivation, or where the population is scattered over a wide area. In such places, more resources will be needed to provide the quality of screening and surveillance that we have specified.

Child health surveillance is a labour-intensive activity and involves very little expenditure on materials or equipment. In some cases, improvements in premises may be needed; for instance, quiet surroundings are essential if hearing tests are to be performed correctly. However, the most important investment is in continuing education for all staff involved in work with children. It will be important to identify funds that can be devoted to this, and in some cases it may be possible to achieve this by the use of existing resources within the community services for children.

We have not attempted to describe individual tests or procedures in detail. There are a number of books which describe the clinical and practical aspects of child health surveillance; details of these are given in the bibliography.

Much remains to be learnt about the tests and procedures used in surveillance. This report can only be a statement of the present situation as perceived by this working party. It is our hope that it will be used not only as a basis for planning current service provision, but also as a stimulus for further research. There is an urgent need for the development of new screening methods, better approaches to evaluation, and studies on service provision.

Our analysis of surveillance was carried out in the context of the health problems, and the services available to deal with them, in Britain during the closing years of the 20th century. Thus we have assumed the continued existence of a network of facilities both in the community and in hospital. Although we feel that the schedule developed here may have implications for other countries, each nation has to consider its major health issues in the light of resources and other competing needs. It would not necessarily be appropriate for others to duplicate our programme precisely. Nevertheless, we hope that our findings may have some relevance to health care overseas.

We wish to thank the British Paediatric Association for providing hospitality for all the meetings of the Working Party and our parent bodies for their encouragement. We are particularly grateful for the interest and support of the DHSS and the Scottish Home and Health Department.

In the Appendix to this volume are listed those individuals and organizations who submitted helpful comments on the first draft of this Report. To them and to all those who made suggestions whether formally or informally, we record our thanks.

July 1988

David Hall
Chairman, Joint Working Party

Contents

List of Members of the Working Party

British Paediatric Association
Dr D.M.B. Hall
Dr J.A. MacFarlane
Professor Catherine Peckham

General Medical Services Committee of the British Medical Association
Dr G. Emrys-Jones
Dr D.J. Godfrey
Dr Alison Hill
Dr D.E. Pickersgill

Health Visitors' Association
Mrs Jan Byrne
Ms Shirley Goodwin
Mrs M. Heal
Ms Rosalynde Lowe
Mrs Alison Norman

Royal College of General Practitioners
Dr S. Carne
Dr P. Evans
Dr D.J. Pereira Gray
Dr W. McN. Styles
Dr C. Waine

Royal College of Nursing
Mrs Ainna Fawcett-Hennessy
Ms Claire Johnston

Additional Invited Members
Dr Anita Jenkins
Dr Marion Miles

Observers
Mr M. Dunning (DHSS)
Mr N. Duncan (DHSS)
Dr Margaret Hennigan (Scottish Health and Home Dept.)
Dr M.G. Wagner (WHO)

1

Surveillance and screening

Scope of this report

Child health surveillance incorporates a wide variety of activities and it would be futile to consider such a complex programme as if it were a single entity. We decided that the only way to proceed was to define the various aims of surveillance and the means by which they might be achieved. Each component could then be analysed in detail.

The working party concentrated on pre-school surveillance, but also, for the sake of continuity, considered selected aspects of surveillance and screening involving children up to school leaving age. We excluded from our deliberations the question of antenatal screening, a topic for which the composition of the working party was inappropriate. For the same reason we did not devote much time to discussion of screening tests based on laboratory procedures.

The working party members were all agreed on the great importance of a properly organized and administered immunization programme[1-3] but thought that since this is the subject of regular comment and review by other expert committees, it would be superfluous to duplicate this in the present report.

Several other organizations and working parties have already considered questions of organization and personnel. The situation has been complicated by the changing relationships within the Health Service between general practitioners, community child health doctors, health visitors and school nurses, and departments of paediatrics based in hospitals. For these reasons, we elected to concentrate on the *content* of the programme and its scientific basis. The aim was to find areas of agreement so that a core programme of surveillance could be established. We would then be able to specify the abilities needed to carry out this programme.

The content of surveillance programmes

The surveillance and monitoring of child health, growth, and development is regarded as good practice throughout the Western World. It has been assumed that the value of these activities is self-evident, but there is a striking paucity of research into the individual tests and other components of the various surveillance programmes.

In the absence of an established scientific base, it is not surprising that there are very wide variations in the pattern of surveillance between countries[4-10]. Even within the UK, there is no uniformity regarding either the number or the content of developmental surveillance examinations[11,12], and detailed enquiries reveal that many Health Authorities are unable either to specify the precise nature of their programme, or to produce evidence of its effectiveness. The differences between districts in the UK cannot be attributed to differing socio-economic conditions.

Individual clinicians have a duty to provide what they regard as optimal care in the light of local conditions. Nevertheless, it should be possible to establish a core programme of surveillance[4] based on considerations of validity and efficiency, which would be acceptable throughout the UK.

Health professionals have differing opinions about the value of surveillance[13-19]. Some believe that every child should undergo seven or more developmental examinations in the pre-school years. At the other extreme are those who claim that surveillance could be abolished without any significant impact on child health and development.

Child health surveillance presents exceptional difficulties for researchers. Screening procedures used to detect disorders among children in the community require validation against standard or reference tests, but the latter are themselves imprecise and often hard to interpret. The situation is further complicated by the difficulty of deciding what constitutes a problem for an individual child and his family and by the uncertainty surrounding the natural history, the value of intervention and the practical significance of many developmental disorders.

Even if all these questions could be answered, it would still be necessary to consider various broader issues; for instance, whether alternative strategies might be equally effective in detection and remediation. Furthermore, since resources are and always will be finite, value judgements must be made about the relative merits of competing health care programmes. In view of the complexity of the issues involved, it is not surprising that our investigations produced more questions than answers.

The need for reappraisal

Recently there has been an increasingly critical approach to all forms of surveillance and screening[20,21]. There are many reasons for this:

1. It is essential to evaluate all health care activities and to define the most cost-effective means of delivering the service.

2. Methodological advances in epidemiology and community medicine have resulted in a more rigorous approach to the evaluation of screening tests.

3. It has been recognized that some screening activities are not merely useless but are potentially harmful because of the unnecessary worry, referrals, and procedures that may result. Indeed, some authorities have argued that it is unethical to offer screening tests that cannot stand up to critical examination.

4. Surveillance, like other aspects of health care, has to be sensitive to the views of the consumer. Parents expect to be

consulted about decisions that involve their children and increasingly are prepared to challenge professional expertise and advice[22].

5. There have also been important changes in education[23]. Since the Education Act of 1981 there has been an increased recognition of the importance of early educational intervention for children with special needs. At the same time there has been a move away from diagnostic labelling or categorization and more emphasis is placed on a descriptive analysis of each child's strengths and weaknesses[24-6].

6. It is thought that too much emphasis has been placed on the detection of defects and too little on preventive and educational activities[27].

It is not possible to make recommendations wholly based on scientific considerations. There are some aspects of child health surveillance that will always be difficult to measure. Our recommendations therefore are based on a combination of research evidence and clinical experience, backed by a commitment to provision of better services for parents and children.

The programme we will recommend at the conclusion of our report should be regarded as a 'best buy' in the light of current evidence. We would anticipate that it will be refined and altered substantially in the light of further research and experience.

2

Definitions and concepts

Since many of the disagreements in the area of child health surveillance arise from problems of terminology, it is important to clarify the terms used[28,29]. The following terms are defined and discussed in this section:

(1) Health promotion
(2) Surveillance
(3) Intervention
(4) Prevention
(5) Health education
(6) Screening
(7) Developmental examination
(8) Developmental screening
(9) Assessment.

Health promotion

Health promotion was described by the World Health Organization[27] as:

the process of enabling people to increase control over, and to improve, their health. To reach a stage of complete physical, mental and social well being, an individual or group must be able to identify and to realise aspirations, to satisfy needs and to change or cope with the environment. Health is, therefore, seen as a resource for everyday life, not the object of living. Health is a positive concept emphasising social and personal resources, as well as physical capacities. Therefore, health promotion is not just the responsibility of the health sector but goes beyond healthy lifestyles to well being.

Thus, health promotion should be regarded as a guiding philosophy rather than a procedure. In the context of child health, it involves an equal constructive partnership between parents and professionals.

Surveillance

Surveillance involves a set of activities which are initiated by professionals. It includes the oversight of the physical, social, and emotional health and development of all children; measurement and recording of physical growth; monitoring of developmental progress; offering and arranging intervention when necessary; prevention of disease by immunization and other means; and health education.

The concept of surveillance is one that involves whole populations. All children should have access to the network of services provided within the surveillance programme, including children with special needs, children of travelling families, those of the homeless, and children of Armed Forces personnel.

Although primary health care professionals have valuable skills and information to offer parents and children, the relationship should not be one of professional supervision but rather a partnership in which parents are enabled to make use of services and expertise in the way that is most appropriate to their needs. For this reason we were uneasy about the suggestion implicit in the term 'surveillance' that the health of children depends on ever-vigilant professionals in a 'Big Brother' role.

Intervention

Intervention means any professional-initiated activity intended to deal with a problem affecting health or development. It includes the therapeutic services provided by primary health care teams, consultants, nurses, health visitors and midwives, speech therapists, psychologists, and other remedial professions. Educational and social work input may be appropriate, and voluntary groups may also contribute.

Prevention

Prevention has three components: primary, secondary, and tertiary. Primary prevention involves precluding the occurrence of disease or injury, for example by immunization programmes. Secondary prevention involves obstructing the development of disease by early detection, for example through screening programmes. Tertiary prevention involves impeding the progress of established disease or disability by appropriate treatment.

Health education

Health education is defined as 'any activity which promotes health-related learning, i.e. some relatively permanent change in an individual's capabilities or dispositions'. Health education is one of the elements by which health promotion may be achieved.

Screening

Screening was defined by the American Commission on Chronic Illness in 1957 as

the presumptive identification of unrecognized disease or defect by the application of tests, examinations, and other procedures, which can be applied rapidly. Screening tests sort out apparently well persons who may have a disease from those who probably do not. A screening test is not intended to be diagnostic.

Criteria for screening programmes

Recognizing that the number of diseases for which screening might in theory be possible is almost unlimited, Wilson and

Yungner[30] devised a set of criteria by which screening programmes could be evaluated:

1. The condition being sought should be an important health problem for the individual and for the community.
2. There should be an acceptable form of treatment for patients with recognizable disease or some other form of useful intervention should be available (e.g. genetic advice).
3. The natural history of the condition, including its development from latent to declared disease, should be adequately understood.
4. There should be a recognizable latent or early symptomatic stage.
5. There should be a suitable test or examination for detecting the disease at an early or latent stage, which should be acceptable to the population.
6. Facilities should be available for diagnosing and treating the patients uncovered by this programme.
7. There should be an agreed policy on whom to treat as patients.
8. The treatment at the pre-symptomatic stage of the disease should favourably influence its course and prognosis.
9. The cost of case finding, which should include cost of diagnosis and treatment, should be economically balanced in relation to (a) possible expenditure on medical care as a whole and (b) the cost of treatment if the patient does not present until the disease reaches the symptomatic stage.
10. Case finding should be a continuing process, not a once and for all project.

Cochrane and Holland[31] described the characteristics of the ideal screening test. It should be:

1. Simple, quick, and easy to interpret: capable of being performed by paramedical or other personnel.
2. Acceptable to the public, since participation in screening programmes is voluntary.

3. Accurate, i.e. give a true measurement of the attribute under investigation.
4. Repeatable. This involves the components of observer variability, both within and between tests; subject variability; and test variability.
5. Sensitive. This is the ability of a test to give a positive finding when the individual screened has the disease or abnormality under investigation.
6. Specific. This is the ability of the test to give a negative finding when the individual does not have the disease or abnormality under investigation.

Rose[32] added the concept of *yield*, which was defined as the number of new, previously unsuspected cases detected per 100 cases screened.

Developmental examination, screening, and assessment

Developmental examination is a term applied to a set of procedures, which usually includes a developmental history, observation of the child's behaviour, and the administration of various tests, in order to establish the stage of development of an individual child and to recognize deviations from normal.

Developmental screening involves the performance of developmental examinations at one or more key ages in apparently normal children. The aim is to examine *all* children in order to identify those who have significant abnormalities that have previously been overlooked. Developmental examination and developmental screening are discussed in more detail in Chapter 11.

Developmental assessment involves the detailed, expert, and often multidisciplinary investigation of manifest or suspected developmental delay or abnormality. In this situation, assessment is a diagnostic and problem-solving exercise.

It is possible to consider assessment in educational rather than medical terms. In this sense it means a continuing process of describing a child's current level of performance, together with strengths and weaknesses, in order to establish an appropriate programme of teaching and to predict likely educational needs in the immediate future. Defined in this way, assessment is not a problem-solving activity, but an intrinsic part of good teaching and indeed of good parental care.

Impairment, disability, and handicap

There is an important distinction between the terms impairment, disability, and handicap. *Impairment* means any abnormality of body structure or function. *Disability* means a reduction in a person's ability to carry out particular tasks, functions or skills. A *handicap* is the effect of the impairment or disability in preventing the individual from pursuing desired aspirations, goals, and roles in society.

3

Early detection

Inevitably, much of our report will focus on the question of early detection, since it is in the area of screening for defects that one finds the greatest variation in standards of practice. Nevertheless, we wish to emphasize that the detection of defects is only one of the aims of the child health service and is by no means the most important.

Does early detection matter?

The working party considered first whether early detection is a legitimate goal for the child health service[33]. It is not possible to give a precise definition of 'early', but the word implies that defects are found at the earliest stage of the disease or disability that is reasonably possible, rather than waiting until they are inescapably obvious. We believe that early detection can be justified on a number of grounds.

In a few disorders, there is no doubt that detection and treatment at the pre-symptomatic stage improve outcome. Examples include phenylketonuria, hypothyroidism, and congenital dislocation of the hip. There are some disorders where it is probable that early detection and treatment improve outcome but the evidence is equivocal. A good example is congenital sensorineural hearing loss. Sometimes early diagnosis permits genetic counselling which may prevent the birth of another child with the same disorder. An example is Duchenne muscular dystrophy.

There are many disorders in which early diagnosis does not reduce the severity of the disability[34,35]. Nevertheless, appropriate intervention enables the child and family to cope with disability more effectively, by reducing parental frustration and isolation, and by helping the child to make the most effective use of any functions and abilities that are preserved. For example, in the case of cerebral palsy, early physiotherapy can prevent or delay the progression of postural deformities and contractures.

Education Authorities need to know about children with special needs, in order to offer pre-school teaching and to enable them to fulfil their responsibilities under the Education Act of 1981. No legal duty has been imposed on Health Authorities to detect children with special needs. There is however a legal requirement for the Health Authority to inform the Education Authority whenever it is suspected that a child may have special educational needs and to inform the parents about any voluntary organization that may be relevant to the child's disability[23,36].

The most compelling reason for early diagnosis is that parents want it. We identified both research evidence and a weight of clinical opinion in favour of this view. Parents feel they have a right to know of any concerns about a child's development at the earliest possible stage. Early diagnosis, if accompanied by adequate counselling, facilitates adaptation and adjustment to the problems created by disability[37-9].

How early detection is achieved

A large proportion of defects and disorders are detected in one of four ways:

(1) the neonatal and six-week examinations;
(2) follow-up of infants and children who have suffered various forms of trauma or illness affecting the nervous system;
(3) detection by parents and relatives;
(4) detection by playgroup leaders, nursery nurses, health visitors, and general practitioners in the course of their regular work.

The neonatal examination and the examination performed at around six weeks of age[40] reveal a significant number of abnormalities, for example dysmorphic conditions such as Down's syndrome, congenital heart disease, and anomalies of the eye[41].

Infants who have suffered illnesses or insults with the potential to cause neurological damage are normally seen regularly in a specialist clinic. A significant proportion of the severely handicapped children known to any Handicap Team are recognized by a paediatrician as being actually or potentially handicapped as soon as the neurological insult occurs. Examples include premature infants who have suffered intraventricular haemorrhage; full-term babies who have suffered hypoxic–ischaemic encephalopathy, neonatal meningitis, or severe hypoglycaemia; and infants and children who have had meningitis, encephalitis, head injury, or encephalopathy.

We are not advocating a return to the concept of an 'at risk' register by which risk factors are recorded with a view to alerting community staff to the possibility of developmental problems[42]. This approach to detection of defects was introduced at a time when resources were very limited and undue emphasis was placed on perinatal factors in the aetiology of developmental disorders and defects. It fell into disrepute for two reasons: it was impossible to obtain consistent reporting and recording of the relevant risk factors; and many children found to have serious handicapping conditions had no antecedent risk factors.

Parents, sometimes with the aid of relatives and friends, are often the first to recognize that their child has a disability. They use their own knowledge and make comparisons with the babies of their friends and relatives, before deciding that their child may not be developing normally. When they report these suspicions to a health professional they often prove to be correct.

The parents are often the first to recognize blindness, cerebral palsy, muscular dystrophy, severe mental handicap, sensorineural deafness, and autism. It is of course true that they frequently fail to understand the significance of their observations but they are very efficient at detecting that something is amiss. Unfortunately, they do not always receive a sympathetic hearing and it is vital that all staff respect and respond to parental worries.

Playgroup leaders and nursery nurses play an increasingly important role in child care, particularly in deprived areas. They become expert at recognizing the child whose health or development requires further evaluation. The value of their contribution should be recognized.

A few defects are detected in the course of a consultation for some other problem. This might be described as 'opportunistic detection'[43,44].

4

The role and value of surveillance

Since the majority of serious defects are detected in the various ways listed above, the working party considered whether there is any need for active surveillance[45]. We concluded that there is such a need, for a number of reasons. A programme of active surveillance provides a framework within which not only the early detection of defects, but also a number of other goals, can be pursued.

Benefits of surveillance

A surveillance programme has several major benefits:

1. Formation of a constructive relationship between professional and family which allows the positive promotion of health, independent of the stress caused by acute medical problems.
2. Preventive work such as immunization and reduction of accident hazards.
3. Guidance on important child health topics such as development, behavioural problems, nutrition, and the use of services for children.
4. Maintenance of a body of knowledge in the community, among both parents and professionals, about child health and development.

Although parents have the key role in the detection of defects, a surveillance programme is nevertheless important. Parents seldom decide instantaneously that their child might have some abnormality of health or development. The conclusion is reached gradually after discussion and observation. Often contact with a professional who has a knowledge of child development enables them to clarify their worries. They can then decide whether and when they wish to obtain more expert advice. Such decisions are not taken lightly. Although most parents are grateful for assessment and support, they are also very anxious about what the outcome will be. They fear that the child may be labelled 'handicapped' or require special education, which for many people still carries a certain stigma[46].

Some parents need help

There is a minority of parents who for a variety of social, psychological, and educational reasons do not recognize or do not understand the significance of the symptoms of illness or of developmental abnormalities. These parents must be treated with sensitivity; the reasons for their lack of awareness are often complex and must be respected. Such parents are found among all social classes and are not confined to the poorly educated or socially deprived[47,48]. The absence of any form of health surveillance might mean that some children could be seriously neglected.

In some circumstances, particularly in conditions of severe social deprivation, parents may acknowledge that their child has some developmental problem such as slow speech development or behaviour disturbance, but may not know how to make use of health, educational, or social services. Active surveillance may make it easier to help such families.

Some defects are difficult to detect

Some defects are unlikely to be recognized even by the most astute parent and will only be detected by health professionals if a specific search is made. Examples include:

(1) congenital dislocation of the hip before the child starts to walk;

(2) high frequency hearing loss prior to the age at which speech normally begins;

(3) amblyopia;

(4) some congenital heart defects.

The detection of such defects can be achieved by the use of specific screening tests. These tests are discussed in Chapters 5–12.

Surveillance is worthwhile

Twenty years ago, it is unlikely that we would have rated so highly the role of parents in detecting problems in their children. Serious abnormalities were commonly overlooked by both parents and professionals until the child started school at the age of five. This distressing occurrence is now quite rare. The improvement is at least partly due to child health surveillance, which provides opportunities to maintain and extend knowledge of child development.

In Chapter 11 we recommend that the *routine developmental examination* of all children should be discontinued. In forming this view we assumed the continued existence of a high standard of *surveillance* available to all children. Without this, there would be a decline in the quality of care available to parents and children and a rise in the average age at which disabilities are diagnosed and intervention is offered. Such a change would be a retrograde step that would be unpopular with parents and would also be contrary to the spirit and intention of the 1981 Education Act.

5

Screening tests

In this section of the report we will undertake a detailed analysis of the screening tests commonly used in child health surveillance. We have attempted to examine each test as if it were being proposed now as a new innovation. In some respects it is more difficult to evaluate a test that has been in routine use for a long time, but this is no reason for not attempting to do so.

In order to standardize our enquiries, the working party adopted an identical format throughout. This is set out in Appendix 1. Space does not allow us to reproduce all the information gathered and only the salient points for each procedure will be discussed.

The various screening tests are grouped together under the following headings:

(1) procedures involving the physical examination (Chapter 6);

(2) laboratory and radiological tests (Chapter 7);

(3) growth monitoring (Chapter 8);

(4) vision testing (Chapter 9);

(5) hearing tests (Chapter 10);

(6) developmental and neurological problems (Chapter 11);

(7) behavioural and psychiatric disorders (Chapter 12).

For each procedure or test, we made an evaluation of its value based on the following classification.

1. The test is of definite value and should be continued, or introduced if not already in use.

2. The test is of uncertain value and may be continued pending further evaluation, but should not be introduced if not already in use.

3. The test is of little or no value and should be discontinued if currently in use.

We did not attempt to specify precisely referral pathways for children who 'fail' screening tests, since the route of referral depends on local resources. However, it is essential that staff know when, where, and how to refer a child who fails a screening test. If this information is not easily available, there is a danger that the child may be subjected to repeated tests that fail to produce a definitive diagnosis, or else is lost to follow-up and never receives appropriate treatment.

6

Physical examination

Neonatal and six-week examinations

A thorough physical examination of every neonate is now
universally accepted as good practice and the whole examination
can be regarded as a screening procedure with a number of
individual components. The yield of this examination is high. It
is accepted and expected by parents, and there seems little doubt
that they value the reassurance of normality at this time. A
second examination at around six weeks of age is generally
thought to be useful, with a smaller but significant yield of
abnormalities.

Both of these examinations are of proven value, though there
is certainly room for considering the precise content and the
nature of the procedures used. No other routine physical examinations are so universally accepted, and therefore we decided
that physical examinations for screening purposes beyond the
age of six to eight weeks would require individual justification.

Recommendations

We recommend the continuation of the neonatal and six- to
eight-week physical examination for every baby.

The following paragraphs consider *individual physical examination procedures* that may be used for screening purposes.

Congenital dislocation of the hip (CDH)

CDH has recently been the subject of a detailed report by an
expert working party[49]. The incidence of unstable hips in the

neonate is 1.5–2 per cent (15–20 per 1000), but of these only 10 per cent become dislocated and a further 10 per cent may show evidence of subluxation or dysplasia. The early detection of CDH is thought to be worthwhile because the response to treatment is better if this is begun before weight-bearing commences[50-3].

The expert working party pointed out that 'it is impossible to detect every CDH at birth . . . and *there must be continuing surveillance until the child is seen to be walking normally'*. Neonatal screening produces a significant number of false positives and overlooks some true cases, even when performed by very experienced examiners. Furthermore, there is evidence that the dislocation may not always be present in the neonatal period. It is therefore important to consider the possibility of CDH whenever a child is seen in the first two years of life[54]. A single neonatal examination is insufficient, but repeated examinations may reduce the incidence of late-diagnosed CDH.

The expert working party listed the following factors which should alert staff to an *increased risk* of CDH: family history, female sex, breech presentation, postural deformities of the feet, caesarean section, oligohydramnios, and fetal growth retardation. They recommended that all infants should have an examination for CDH *at the following times*: within 24 hours of birth; at the time of discharge from hospital or within 10 days of birth; at six weeks of age; at six to nine months; 15–21 months. The gait should be reviewed at 24–30 months and again at pre-school or school entry examination.

The Ortolani/Barlow manoeuvre should be used for the first three examinations but is not appropriate after the age of three months. Classic signs of CDH should be sought at all examinations. The gait should be observed once the child is walking.

Comment on report of expert working party

It would be superfluous for us to consider the subject of CDH examinations further in detail, but we wish to make four observations:

1. Much remains to be learnt about the natural history of CDH and there have been some criticisms of the currently recommended screening programmes[53,55]. In particular, there is concern about the poor specificity and sensitivity of the neonatal examination.

2. Because of the trend towards early discharge from hospital, it is increasingly difficult to ensure that the second check for CDH is carried out. It will be necessary to determine whether the yield of new cases is sufficient to justify this recommendation and if so to consider what arrangements are needed.

3. An examination at 15–21 months does not coincide conveniently with any other examination which we would wish to recommend. We would prefer to describe this examination as taking place between 18 and 24 months in order to fit in with the rest of the schedule which we will be suggesting.

4. Children with neurological disease, particularly those with spastic cerebral palsy, are at high risk of dislocation of the hip throughout childhood and should be under the supervision of a specialist clinic.

Recommendations

The working party recognizes that the screening programme for CDH is one that must continue. We endorse the schedule recommended by the expert working party above, except that an examination at 18–24 months should replace the last two in that schedule.

Further research

Further research into the CDH examination is required. It will be important to monitor the yield of the expanded screening programme recommended by the expert working party, in order to determine whether the increased emphasis on *repeated examinations* will lead to a reduction in the number of late diagnoses (i.e. diagnoses made only after the child begins to walk).

Ultrasound examination of the hip joint may be a more effective way of diagnosing congenital hip disorders[56]. It is still in the research and development stage and there are likely to be considerable problems regarding finance, personnel, training, and organization before it could be introduced as a universal screening programme. It may however be the key to a better understanding of the natural history of CDH, which must be acquired before a more rational approach to screening can be developed.

Congenital heart disease

The incidence of congenital heart disease (CHD) in the UK is said to be 0.55 to 0.59 per cent (5.5 to 5.9 per thousand)[57]. The incidence of symptomatic CHD in infancy is 0.26 per cent (2.6 per thousand).

Early detection

Early detection of CHD is desirable for three reasons:

1. Deterioration may be rapid and catastrophic and the outcome may be better if the infant is investigated before this occurs.
2. If the diagnosis is missed in the first few weeks of life, because the infant is asymptomatic, the defect may not present until irreversible changes have occurred—for example, pulmonary hypertension in children with left to right shunt.
3. Even defects that are trivial in haemodynamic terms may predispose to endocarditis if antibiotic prophylaxis is not recommended for dental and other procedures.

The main screening test for CHD is the *clinical examination*[58-61]. (A few cases may be recognized antenatally by ultrasound examination). The recognition of cyanosis and respiratory distress together with the detection of murmurs are the main pointers to CHD in the first few weeks of life. The importance of persistent tachypnoea is insufficiently appreciated and it is too often assumed that the absence of a significant murmur rules out heart disease. Other important symptoms include slow feeding, failure to thrive, and repeated chest infections.

The working party could find no clear guidelines on the precise age at which auscultation of the heart should be undertaken as a screening examination. The majority of children who eventually need surgery present in infancy, but some cases of asymptomatic CHD may be detected by routine examinations. It is often assumed that murmurs are the only significant auscultatory finding (see below), but there are other physical signs which might indicate asymptomatic heart disease. Some of these are quite subtle and are only likely to be detected if a high standard of clinical examination is maintained; for instance, ejection clicks and fixed splitting of the second heart sound. If coarctation does not present in the first few weeks of life, it is likely to be overlooked unless the femoral pulses are always examined carefully.

Innocent murmurs

The commonest problem regarding routine auscultation of the heart is the difficulty experienced by non-specialist staff in distinguishing innocent from pathological murmurs[58]. Innocent murmurs are very common, occurring in 50 per cent or more of children. Where there is doubt, expert consultation and/or echocardiography are preferable to leaving parents in a state of uncertainty. Parents must be told what is meant by an innocent murmur.

Down's syndrome

Children with Down's syndrome constitute a special case[62]. Approximately 50 per cent have congenital heart disease, not always accompanied by significant murmurs, and the progression to irreversible pulmonary hypertension is unusually rapid. Diagnosis of clinically inapparent defects is assisted by an ECG and an echocardiogram. Parents must not be wrongly reassured that their child has a normal heart.

Recommendations

Careful auscultation of the heart should be undertaken in the neonate and at six to eight weeks of age, and on at least one occasion thereafter between six weeks and five years of age. The latter recommendation does not necessarily imply a special consultation for this purpose; auscultation may be performed during the course of an examination undertaken for some other purpose.

In teaching, the importance of tachypnoea, the auscultation of the second sound, and the features which distinguish innocent murmurs should be emphasized.

Every infant with Down's syndrome should have an ECG as well as the usual clinical examination. Ideally they should also have an echocardiogram.

Hypertension

Screening for asymptomatic elevation of blood pressure[63-5] could be justified on two grounds. First, it will allow detection of *secondary hypertension*, due for example to coarctation of the aorta, endocrine disorders, or silent renal disease, at a stage before the child presents with serious symptoms such as encephalopathy or vision disturbances. The incidence of symptomatic hypertension is less than 0.1 per cent (1 in 1000).

Second, a screening programme would also detect children with *mild elevation of blood pressure*, who have an increased risk of developing essential hypertension in adult life. They could be advised to make appropriate changes in diet, weight, and life style (though there is as yet no evidence that such advice would be either acceptable or effective).

The main argument against screening is that there is no clear distinction between normal and elevated readings and therefore an arbitrary cut-off point for referral has to be selected. Many children with mild elevations of blood pressure must be identified and investigated in order to detect the few cases of secondary hypertension. Since the former group cannot be offered any simple treatment programme for proven effectiveness, there is at present a substantial risk that the harm done by producing anxiety may exceed any possible benefits.

In an American study on community screening the examination of 10 000 children did not yield a single case of secondary hypertension and no case with primary or essential hypertension was found in which it was thought justifiable to embark on drug treatment[66]. The authors of the study, and subsequently the USA Task Force on screening, concluded that at the present time screening for hypertension in childhood cannot be recommended. (It should however be noted that in the USA children are examined more frequently by their personal physician than is the case in the UK and hypertension might therefore be diagnosed at an earlier stage even without a screening programme.)

Recommendations

We recommend that at present no attempt should be made to introduce universal screening for hypertension. Further research on the detection of secondary hypertension and the prevention of essential hypertension may change this view in the near future[67]. Measurement of the blood pressure must be part of the clinical evaluation of any child presenting with a relevant medical problem.

Respiratory disease

The most important condition to be considered here is asthma[68] (cystic fibrosis is considered in Chapter 7). Symptoms of asthma may begin in the first year of life[69]. By the age of five years, 10–12 per cent of children have episodic or persistent wheezing; in some cases the main feature may be exercise-induced wheeze or nocturnal cough. There is sometimes a reluctance on the part of medical staff to label the condition as asthma, but it is important to make the correct diagnosis so that appropriate treatment can be given, unnecessary antibiotics avoided, and absences from school reduced[70-4].

There is no formal screening test for asthma in common use, although for research purposes a questionnaire has been found to be a satisfactory way of identifying the condition. A key question is 'Has your child ever had one or more attacks of wheezing?' It is said that 96 per cent of cases can be identified by this simple question[73].

Recommendations

Our recommendation at present is that awareness about the high prevalence of mild asthma is more important than a structured screening programme. Any parent who is concerned about their child's respiratory symptoms should be asked about wheezing.

Further research

Further research is needed into screening for asthma. It would be possible to 'screen' all school entrants by asking the key question mentioned above, but further work is needed to determine the acceptability of such a programme and the possible benefits (and hazards) of treatment on symptoms, hospitalization and time off school. It is clear that the increased awareness of asthma results in more use of paediatric hospital services and this issue requires urgent investigation. An exercise test may be an alternative method of screening[75].

Abnormalities of the genitalia

Careful inspection of the genitalia in the neonate is an essential part of the routine neonatal examination. It should be possible at this age to detect the majority of serious disorders. By far the commonest problem detectable by screening examination is abnormal descent of the testicle. At birth, 6.0 per cent (60 per 1000) of males have one or both testes undescended and the rate is some five times higher in low birth-weight babies as compared to full-term infants[76].

A high proportion of testes undescended at birth have descended normally by three months of age. The prevalence at this age is 1.6 per cent (16 per 1000). Further natural descent is unlikely after three months of age. Some testes apparently normally descended at three months may be found to be incompletely descended when re-examined between one and five years of age. The majority of these boys have had late initial descent of the testes between birth and three months of age or were thought to have incomplete initial descent at the first examination.

Infant boys suspected of having incomplete descent of the testis should if possible be referred for surgical opinion before the age of 18 months because early surgery may improve fertility, and facilitate the early diagnosis of malignancy[77-81].

The screening test is a physical examination[82]. The testis is gently manipulated into the lowest position along the pathway of normal anatomical descent without tension being applied. The most precise criterion for diagnosis of undescended testis at birth and in the first few months of life is that the centre of at least one testis should be less than 4 cm below the pubic tubercle, or 2.5 cm in babies weighing under 2.5 kg. Subjective classification by experienced examiners into three categories (well down, high scrotal, or suprascrotal) is as reliable as actual measurement.

It is sometimes difficult to distinguish between maldescent and retractile testis, particularly in the three to five age group. Previous records may be helpful. The decision to undertake orchidopexy should be made by an experienced surgeon; there is evidence that some orchidopexies are performed for retractile testes.

Recommendations

We recommend that:

1. A note should be made of testicular descent at the neonatal examination. Further examinations are particularly import-

ant in those cases where the testis is *not* 'well down' in the scrotum.

2. A further check should be made at around eight months of age and if there is doubt about the descent of either or both testes at this age, the child should be referred for surgical opinion. When the testes *are* completely descended, this should be recorded and the parent should be told.

3. Since it appears that late ascent of a previously descended testis may occur, a further check should be made between three and five years of age, particularly in cases where there was doubt about testicular descent in the early months of life.

4. These checks are often neglected in children who are handicapped. *All* children should be examined.

5. The number of boys discovered to have an untreated undescended testis at the age of five or subsequently could be recorded as a measure of the success in screening for undescended testes, though the number of orchidopexies performed would only be a reliable means of monitoring if the precautions mentioned previously are observed.

Adolescent scoliosis

This disorder appears after the age of 10 and it is much commoner for progression to serious deformity to occur in girls. The estimated incidence of scoliosis needing treatment is around 0.3 per cent (3 per 1000). Mild curves which do not progress are very much commoner. When progression does occur it compromises pulmonary and cardiac function and leads to severe cosmetic deformity[83].

Bracing at an early stage may reduce the need for surgery, which is a worthwhile achievement because the operations required are extensive and have a significant morbidity and mortality.

The forward bending test has been extensively used for screening adolescent girls. This test is too sensitive, resulting in referral of between 2 and 15 per cent of children screened. Many of the mild curves thus detected do not progress, but repeated radiology and examination are required to monitor each patient. The unnecessary treatment of perhaps two out of every three children treated is likely to result from such a screening programme.

If these problems could be overcome there would be considerable advantages in screening for adolescent scoliosis[84-9], but the Natural History Committee of the British Scoliosis Society does not recommend that at the present time the screening of adolescents for scoliosis should be routine policy in the United Kingdom. The development of the 'scoliometer' may overcome some of the current difficulties.

Recommendations

Screening programmes currently in existence should continue, *provided that* data is being gathered that will be useful in further evaluation of screening programmes. New screening programmes should not be introduced at the present time.

All health care staff should be aware of the possible significance of scoliosis and of the need to refer such cases promptly for orthopaedic opinion.

The Natural History Committee of the British Scoliosis Society should be asked to maintain a regular liaison with the organizations represented on this working party, regarding further research on screening programmes for scoliosis.

7

Laboratory and radiological
screening tests

In general, screening procedures requiring laboratory or radiological tests have been subjected to more critical evaluation than
clinical examinations, presumably because of the obvious costs
involved and the requirements for careful organization. We have
therefore devoted relatively little time to this topic.

Phenylketonuria and hypothyroidism

Screening programmes for phenylketonuria (PKU) and hypothyroidism are now well established. Their value appears to be
beyond dispute and although they are expensive they are thought
to be cost-effective[90].

It will never be possible to screen 100 per cent of the population and no laboratory test can ever be totally reliable. The
diagnoses of PKU and hypothyroidism should always be considered in appropriate clinical circumstances. The results of the
screening test should be seen and recorded and there should be
no hesitation in repeating the investigations whenever there is
doubt. This is particularly important in the case of hypothyroidism[91-2]. The screening procedure is known to miss up to 7 per
cent of cases, but it is not considered cost-effective to undertake
a second screening test. The increased incidence of hypothyroidism in Down's syndrome and in some ethnic groups should be
remembered[93,94].

Other genetic disorders

Screening for other inborn errors of metabolism is possible and is being investigated both in some parts of the UK and also overseas. Examples of conditions whose early detection may be both useful and cost-effective include galactosaemia, maple syrup urine disease, homocystinuria, medium-chain acylCoA dehydrogenase deficiency, and biotinidase deficiency.

Screening for cystic fibrosis[95,96] and Duchenne muscular dystrophy[97] in the neonatal period has been advocated but for various reasons has not been widely adopted. Screening for cystic fibrosis would permit very early detection, so that treatment could begin before lung damage had occurred.

It is technically possible to screen all boys for Duchenne muscular dystrophy at birth. The advantage of early diagnosis would be that the birth of further affected boys could be avoided[98,99]. The main argument against this procedure has been that the total number of births thus prevented would be very small, so that the procedure might not justify its cost. An alternative approach is to screen all boys who first walk later than 18 months, since 50 per cent of cases are late walkers. This policy has not been adopted, because the yield is likely to be 1 per cent or less and there are serious logistic problems.

DNA technology

Although screening has been introduced in some parts of the country using currently available techniques, knowledge of these conditions is advancing so rapidly that it would seem unwise to recommend the introduction of universal screening at this time. Districts and health boards should be aware that DNA technology may greatly extend the feasibility of and demand for such screening in the next few years.

Recommendations

At the present time we recommend only that a high level of awareness is maintained regarding the presenting features of these conditions. Suspect cases should be referred for the appropriate diagnostic tests without hesitation.

Urine examination as a screening test

Screening for proteinuria and for asymptomatic bacteriuria has been advocated in the past on the grounds that chronic pyelonephritis resulting in chronic renal failure might be a preventable condition. We could find no convincing evidence that this is a worthwhile procedure[100] and **do not recommend it.**

Screening for haemoglobinopathies

The two most important haemoglobinopathies are sickle cell disease and the thalassaemias, though there are a number of other less common abnormal haemoglobins[101,102].

Approximately 3.3 per cent of the total UK population belongs to a racial group with a significant risk of having an abnormal haemoglobin. One person in 80 of West African origin and one in 200 of Jamaican origin has sickle cell disease. There are said to be approximately 4000–5000 sickle cell disease sufferers in the UK and about 70 babies are born with the condition each year. In the UK there are an estimated 350 people with thalassaemia major and about 60 children are born each year with the condition.

Importance of early diagnosis

There is a significant morbidity and mortality from sickle cell disease, particularly in the first three years of life. Sickle cell disease is associated with impaired immunity and fulminating pneumococcal infection. This can be prevented by penicillin prophylaxis, which needs to be started by four months of age. Parents can be taught to recognize splenic sequestration crises[103-5].

Children with thalassaemia usually present with anaemia and failure to thrive. These features should lead to early diagnosis, followed by treatment with blood transfusion and iron chelation therapy.

The need for a screening programme

A neonatal screening programme would aim to reduce the morbidity and mortality rates of infants born with haemoglobinopathies. Antenatal screening and advice might be followed by fetal diagnosis and termination of affected pregnancies if the parents so wished[106,107].

Screening for haemoglobinopathies is a complex undertaking, involving obstetric, haematological, genetic, and paediatric services. Skilled counsellors are essential and there are some difficult ethical problems. Nevertheless, such a service is likely to be cost-effective and there is evidence that it would be acceptable to and well used by the ethnic minorities involved[108,109].

Recommendations

The composition of the present working party was not appropriate for the specialized task of advising in detail on further developments in this field. However, a strong case can be made for the establishment of a screening programme for haemoglobinopathies and we recommend that any such initiatives should be supported and encouraged.

Iron deficiency anaemia

This is a common disorder in the age range six months to four years, with an apparent peak at around three years and an average prevalence of 5 to 10 per cent[110]. It can be detected by investigating all children with an Hb concentration of less than 11 g dl^{-1} between six months and six years. The ill effects of iron deficiency anaemia are probably related to the lack of iron rather than the low haemoglobin. These effects are said to include behavioural difficulties, developmental deficits, and an increased susceptibility to infections[111-14].

Iron deficiency can be defined more precisely by a transferrin saturation of less than 16 per cent, a serum iron of less than 14 μmol l^{-1}, a TIBC of less than 40 μmol l^{-1}, or a serum ferritin of less than 12 ng ml^{-1}.

Causes

Iron deficiency is more common in the underprivileged and in ethnic minorities. Causes include inadequate dietary content of foods containing iron, the use of fresh cows milk, drinking tea (which chelates iron) and a number of other factors have also been suggested.

Treatment

Iron deficiency is easily treated with a one or two month course of oral iron[115,116]. This is well tolerated and there is no evidence of any significant risk attached to such treatment, except for the risk of poisoning by overdose or accidental ingestion by other children and the remote possibility of increasing iron overload in a case of undiagnosed thalassaemia.

The evidence suggests that iron deficiency is a significant health problem in young children. An Hb measurement of less than 11 g dl^{-1} could be used as an indirect screening test, since direct measures of iron status are more technically demanding. Hb can be measured using capillary blood samples and a haemoglobinometer.

Recommendations

Although screening for iron deficiency is certainly possible and probably desirable, published evidence allows us to make only one firm recommendation. All staff need to be aware that iron deficiency is a very common disorder and one that is easily treated. There should be no hesitation about obtaining an Hb estimation and where necessary giving a therapeutic trial of iron.

Further research

Further research on screening for iron deficiency anaemia is needed. Questions to be considered include:

1. Whether routine blood sampling would be acceptable to parents.
2. Whether the incidence of iron deficiency could be reduced by appropriate health education (see also page 84).
3. What measurable benefits might result from a more aggressive approach to the identification and treatment of iron deficiency.

Familial hypercholesterolaemia

This is a dominantly inherited disorder with an incidence of 0.1–0.2 per cent (1 in 500–1 in 1000)[117-20]. It carries a higher risk of early heart disease than does polygenic hypercholesterolaemia. It is not feasible at present to screen all children for this condition or for the other hyperlipidaemias. We **recommend** that screening for hypercholesterolaemia should be confined to the families of known sufferers from this condition and to the relatives, including children, of any person suffering coronary heart disease at a young age (i.e. below 50 years of age for a male and below 60 for a female).

Atlanto-axial instability in people with Down's syndrome

This condition is commoner in females and the overall rate has been variously reported at between 12 and 22 per cent[121]. Rarely, it may be associated with cervical cord damage. It has been suggested that there is an increased risk of cord compression for those who participate in vigorous sports (especially trampolining or high board diving) and from hyperextension of the neck during anaesthesia. A DHSS working party identified very few cases in the world literature and a significant proportion of these followed whiplash injury in road traffic accidents. In many cases the onset is insidious rather than acute and can be identified by alteration in the tendon reflexes.

Screening for atlanto-axial instability has been recommended using X-rays of the spine to measure the atlanto-odontoid interval. The interpretation of these X-rays is often difficult and **we do not recommend this** as a method of screening.

We recommend that people with Down's syndrome should always wear seat belts when travelling by car, whether in the front or rear of the vehicle.

Further research is needed to ascertain the most appropriate policy for screening, either on a regular routine basis or prior to anaesthesia.

8

Growth monitoring

It is important to be sure that growth monitoring in children is being properly utilized and is not doing more harm than good. The routine measurement of height, weight, and head circumference (HC) is a widely accepted practice, but there is no uniformity in the ages at which measurements are made or recorded. The interpretation of the measurements requires some skill, and inappropriate referrals can generate both excessive anxiety and a substantial increase in specialist workload.

Weight

Regular weighing

Although regular weighing cannot be regarded as a screening procedure, it is valued by parents and is used by them as a focus for visits to the clinic or surgery. It seems likely that the procedure of weighing a baby has some social value, in that the baby's weight is used as a discussion point regarding nutrition and other aspects of child rearing.

Failure to thrive

Regular weighing of babies may be useful both to detect abnormalities, and more importantly, to reassure the mother that the child is thriving. In practice, however, it is rare that the weight chart is the only clue to a serious abnormality affecting growth. Unless other symptoms or signs are present as well, the investigation of infants who fail to thrive seldom reveals any significant organic disease. Rapid downwards crossing of the centiles, weight loss, or prolonged failure to gain any weight suggests the presence of pathology. However, most of the babies who gain weight slowly or whose weight graph gradually crosses centile lines downwards are in fact normal. They are simply adopting their own genetically determined growth trajectory and it should not be assumed that every baby will continue on the same centile from birth onwards.

Weight may fluctuate by several hundred grams, depending on the contents of bowel, bladder, and stomach as well as minor fluctuations due to intercurrent illness. Static weight for a week or two and even transient weight loss are common.

Other reasons have been advanced in support of regular weighing:

1. Psychosocial factors are sometimes responsible for poor weight gain, which in this situation is known as 'non-organic failure to thrive'[122,123]. Regular weighing may facilitate detection of these children who are 'at risk' not only of continued poor growth but also of significant developmental problems[124-6]. In the more severe cases there is also a decline in the rate of increase of head circumference and in height velocity.

2. It has been suggested that an intervention programme that includes regular weighing of babies identified by health visitors as being 'at risk' may reduce the incidence of sudden unexpected death in infancy[127-9].

We regard as outdated the view that infant obesity is an important risk factor for adult obesity and we do not think it necessary to comment adversely on the fact that a baby's weight is around or above the 97th centile or on the appearance of plumpness except in extreme cases[130,131].

When parents or other relatives are anxious about their child's weight or food intake in the second and third years of life, plotting the child's weight on a chart may be useful as a way of reassuring them. As a routine procedure however we can see no justification for weighing each child beyond the first year of life.

Conclusions

We found little evidence on which to base any firm conclusions. There seems to have been little evaluation of growth monitoring as performed in child health clinics and this is an important area for further study. We were not convinced that the advantages conferred by regular weighing justify the resources required or the anxiety generated by inexpert interpretation of growth charts. However, in view of its apparent popularity with parents and the opinions mentioned above, it would be premature to recommend that the practice be discontinued.

Recommendations

We recommend the following:

1. Each baby should be weighed at each clinic visit, or at the mother's request.
2. The baby should be weighed nude unless there are special circumstances (e.g. a dressing or splint). In this case, the state of dress should be recorded.
3. The scales should be checked and calibrated regularly.
4. All measurements should be entered on a suitable growth chart. Correction for gestational age is essential.
5. Measurements should be dated, recorded in figures as well as a point on the graph, and signed.
6. All growth charts used in clinics should include both the third centile line and the minus 3SD line. (NB three standard deviations indicates a measurement which differs very substantially from the mean and is therefore likely to be associated with a significant abnormality).
7. Training in the interpretation of growth charts is essential.

Further research

Research needs include further studies of the advantages and disadvantages of regular weighing in terms of abnormalities and problems discovered or prevented, referrals generated with their outcome, and parents' perceptions. In particular, we need to evaluate the relevance of regular weighing to detect psychosocial deprivation and to prevent unexpected death in infancy.

Height measurements

Up to the age of two years it is usual to measure supine length, using a commercially available measuring device. Accurate equipment is expensive but it is impossible to obtain reliable length measurements by any other means. After the age of two years, standing height should be measured. Some two-year-olds are upset by the procedure and a reliable measurement cannot always be obtained, but most three-year-olds can be measured without difficulty.

There are several devices for measuring height.* A simple screening chart can be used to detect those children who need more detailed measurement. Its main disadvantage is that for those children who 'pass' the screening test, no height measurement is recorded for future reference. Cheap measuring sticks, often mounted on weighing scales, are inaccurate. Measurement errors can be as much as 1–2 cm. For clinic or school use, the best results are obtained with a microtoise or with a magnetic measuring device. Specialist clinics use a more expensive device which in the hands of trained staff can produce readings repeatable to within 0.2 cm.

Height velocity is estimated by calculating the increase in height over a specified time interval, which must not be less than six months. The velocity varies with age and it is not possible to specify a single figure to separate normal from suspect height

* Details are available from the Child Growth Foundation

velocity. The calculated figure should be plotted on a chart showing the centiles for height velocity; some charts also indicate the range in which referrals should be considered.

The value of height monitoring

Measurement of length or height is potentially useful for the following reasons[132-4].

1. It is an important part of growth monitoring in cases where some abnormality is suspected, for example in an infant who at birth was noted to be very small for dates, or who is thought to be failing to thrive, or who has a dysmorphic syndrome. Children who suffered from intrauterine growth retardation often continue to grow at a lower than normal velocity. Research is currently being undertaken to assess possible ways of treating these children.

2. It permits the early detection of conditions which limit growth; for example, growth hormone deficiency[135], hypothyroidism, and Turner's syndrome[136]. The incidence of juvenile hypothyroidism is 1 in 3000, that of growth hormone deficiency 1 in 3–5000. Turner's syndrome occurs in 1 in 2500 females.

Growth impairment can be the presenting feature of many other disorders. The majority are likely to be associated with other symptoms, but short stature may be the only sign of conditions such as inflammatory bowel disease or chronic renal failure.

3. Some forms of bone dysplasia can present with short stature, but without other obvious disproportion in the early stages. Diagnosis is important because genetic counselling may be required and new possibilities for treatment are being investigated.

4. Growth monitoring might also be useful as a means of detecting excessively tall stature.

Measurement

The screening test is the measurement itself. This must be plotted on a suitable chart. There is no specific cut-off point between normal and abnormal measurements. Three per cent of children are by definition below the third centile in height (and 3 per cent are above the 97th centile). The majority of short children are normal children of short parents. A pathological cause for short stature is much more likely to be present if successive measurements show a fall in growth velocity, or if the initial measurement is below the -3 SD line on the chart.

We are doubtful about the value of measuring the length in the neonate except in cases of suspected growth retardation or other abnormality. It has even been suggested that the extension of the hips needed to measure length accurately in the neonate might increase the risk of hip dislocation.

We could find no evidence to support the routine measurement of length in the first year of life, though clearly this should be undertaken if some growth disorder is suspected. Measurement between 12 and 24 months of age might facilitate the early diagnosis of growth disorders, but it is difficult to obtain accurate measurements without distressing the child and is therefore not recommended as a routine procedure. The optimum age for a measurement of height as a universal screening procedure is around the third birthday.

Recommendations

We recommend the following procedure as the most efficient approach to the problem at the present time.

1. A height measurement should be made and recorded at around three years of age, or sooner if a suitable opportunity is presented and the child is sufficiently co-operative to permit reliable measurement.

2. If the height measurement is below the -3 SD line, specialist opinion should be considered.

3. If it is below the third centile but above the -3 SD line, the most likely cause is parental short stature. The heights of the parents should be obtained and these measurements used to decide whether parental size is an adequate explanation for the child's short stature. Techniques are available to increase the precision of this comparison.

4. If there is any concern that there may be some other explanation, a further measurement should be made not less than six months later.

5. A further measurement of height should be made between four and five years of age. If the height is below the third centile or a significant shift across centiles is suspected, a further measurement should be made not less than six months later.

6. Height measurements beyond the age of five should also be made (a) if there is doubt about the significance of measurements already obtained, or (b) if previous records are incomplete or unsatisfactory.

7. A further opinion should be considered where there is doubt after two measurements.

8. At present, it would not be realistic to recommend the use of height velocity charts in screening, although the ability to calculate and interpret growth velocity would undoubtedly increase the efficiency of the screening process.

9. An understanding of the technique of accurate height measurement, the use and interpretation of growth charts, and the indications for referral is essential.

Further research

Research is needed to determine the efficiency and effectiveness of the approach we have suggested. The role of height velocity charts in screening needs to be investigated, as does the most appropriate equipment. The reliability of routine measurement of height in two-year-old children and the value of continued monitoring after school entry, should be tested.

Head circumference (HC)

A routine measurement of head circumference is intended to aid the detection of two groups of disorders, those characterized by a large head, and those indicated by a small head. These conditions cannot be diagnosed by measurement of the head circumference alone[137,138]. Since three per cent of children have a head circumference above the 97th centile and three per cent are below the third centile, other evidence must be sought to determine whether a particular measurement is significant.

Conditions with enlargement of the head include hydrocephalus, subdural effusion and haematoma, and a number of less common conditions associated with dysmorphic syndromes etc.

Hydrocephalus is characterized by a head measurement that is crossing centile lines upwards, together with the well-known features of suture separation, tense fontanel, prominent veins, downward gaze, irritability, and sometimes developmental abnormalities. A much commoner cause of head enlargement is a familial large head, in which the growth line may cross centiles but the other symptoms are usually absent.

An abnormally small head is designated microcephaly. This may arise from some abnormality of brain development in the pregnancy, or may be a sign of impaired brain growth due to some peri- or post-natal insult. Very rarely it is associated with craniostenosis. Usually this condition results in an abnormally shaped head. A small but normally shaped head results only from total craniostenosis which is extremely rare and usually associated with other symptoms and signs.

Microcephaly cannot be defined by any absolute cut-off point. Head measurements well below the third centile are compatible with normal intellect. The probability of abnormality is much higher if the measurement is below the -3 SD line. Some ethnic groups tend to have small head measurements, and the use of growth charts not designed for them can be misleading.

Early treatment for hydrocephalus is desirable[139], though there is no conclusive evidence that it improves outcome. There is no specific treatment for microcephaly.

Recommendations

We recommend that the head circumference should be recorded before discharge from hospital following birth. This is an important measurement and should be performed and recorded carefully. If there is excessive oedema or moulding of the scalp following birth this fact should also be recorded and if possible the measurement should be repeated a few days later. Head measurement should subsequently be undertaken at approximately six weeks of age. It should be plotted on the chart and also written in figures. If there is no concern at this time no further routine measurements are needed, but the HC should always be measured and recorded if there is any concern about a baby's growth, health, or development.

If the growth line is crossing the centiles upwards, and the child shows symptoms or signs compatible with hydrocephalus or other abnormality, specialist opinion is essential. If there are no accompanying symptoms or signs, two measurements over a four-week period are acceptable. Beyond this time limit, a decision must be made either to accept the situation as normal (usually on the basis of the fact that the baby is big and that the parents have big heads), or alternatively the child should be referred for specialist examination. There is no justification for repeated measurements spread over many months, a practice which is to be deplored because it creates excessive anxiety. Modern imaging techniques make it simple to obtain a definitive diagnosis at an early stage.

A head measurement above or below the ±3 SD line at any stage is an indication for more detailed assessment. There is an important exception: in some ethnic groups a small head may be a reflection of genetic characteristics and the parents' head measurements should always be checked. If they also are small and the baby appears to be developing normally referral may not be necessary. If the growth line crosses centiles downwards but the baby is otherwise well and thriving, no special arrangements need be made. Concern should be expressed to the parents only if it becomes clear that the growth line is not only below the third percentile but is also falling away from it.

These apparently straightforward monitoring procedures must not be regarded as simple screening tests. Skill and judgement are required in deciding how to interpret the measurements and no single pass/fail criterion can be proposed.

Research needs

Little is known about the accuracy, value or optimal timing of regular head circumference measurement or the relative merits of different referral criteria. Both these subjects require further investigation.

9

Screening for vision defects

Disorders of vision can be sub-divided into the following categories:

1. Serious defects likely to cause a disabling impairment of vision, ranging from partial sight to complete blindness[140].
2. The common and usually less disabling defects, including refractive errors, squints, and amblyopia.
3. Defects of colour discrimination.

Partial sight and blindness

Conditions causing a disabling vision impairment are individually and collectively uncommon[141], with a combined incidence between two and four cases per 10 000 births. This figure is however likely to be an underestimate, because there is under reporting of vision defects in children with multiple handicaps.

Early detection of severe defects

Early detection of serious visual impairment is important for four reasons. First, a few conditions are surgically treatable, for example cataract[142], glaucoma, and retinoblastoma. Second, many visual disorders have genetic implications. Third, developmental guidance to the parents regarding the progress of partially sighted or blind children is much appreciated and probably reduces the incidence of secondary disabilities such as behaviour problems[143]. Finally, visual failure is occasionally the presenting feature of serious systemic disease.

Many cases are detected by parents or other family members[41]. A significant number are found at the neonatal examination, by simple inspection of the eyes. Some are found by specialist examination of known high risk groups, including low birthweight infants at risk of retinopathy of prematurity, and babies with a first degree relative known to have a potentially heritable eye disorder.

Recommendations

Regarding the detection of severe visual impairment, we make the following recommendations.

1. A careful inspection of the eyes is a mandatory part of the neonatal examination. Fundoscopy is not essential but the ophthalmoscope may be used with a $+3$ lens from a distance of 8–12 inches, to detect a cataract as a silhouette against the red reflex. If there is any doubt about the adequacy of the neonatal examination, the inspection and the examination should be repeated at six weeks.

2. The parents should be asked if there is a family history of visual disorders. Children at risk of having a genetically determined disabling visual disorder should be examined with extra care, preferably by an ophthalmologist.

3. Parents should be asked soon after the birth and at each subsequent contact whether they have any anxieties about the baby's vision. Specifically, they should be asked if the baby looks at the parents, follows moving objects with the eyes, and fixates on small objects.

4. All staff should be familiar with the visual development of the normal baby, and should be alert to the various symptoms and signs which first warn parents that there may be a visual defect: for example, abnormal appearance of the eyes, wandering eye movements, poor fixation and visual following, photophobia etc.

5. Children with other major defects affecting the nervous system should undergo a specialist eye examination.

6. It should be remembered that poor visual fixation in the first year of life is sometimes the presenting feature of mental handicap rather than of an eye disorder.

Common vision defects

Definitions

Before discussing the question of screening for the common, less disabling defects, it is necessary to define and discuss the following terms[144]:

(1) visual acuity;

(2) refractive error;

(3) amblyopia;

(4) manifest squint;

(5) latent squint.

Visual acuity is a measure of how well a person is able to separate adjacent visual stimuli. With the exception of a few laboratory procedures, its measurement requires the subject's co-operation. The standard by which all other measures of visual acuity are judged is the Snellen Letter Chart.

A refractive error is a disturbance of the optical system of the eye, such that a sharp image is not formed precisely on the retina. The direct measurement of refractive error involves the technique of retinoscopy, which needs considerable skill. Cycloplegic agents must be instilled in the eye to paralyse accommodation.

Few eyes form a perfect optical system and most people have some refractive error, which may change considerably in infancy and continue to alter throughout life. The decision as to when a refractive error should be regarded as abnormal depends on clinical expertise and judgement.

The correction of impaired visual acuity related to refractive error usually involves the prescription of spectacles. Severely impaired visual acuity may affect school work and sporting prowess, but minor impairments caused by slight refractive errors seem to have little impact on education or performance. Children are often reluctant to wear spectacles prescribed for these minor errors[145].

A manifest squint is a squint that is apparent at the time of examination. It is demonstrated by use of the cover test. The prevalence of squint in childhood is between 3 and 7 per cent.

A latent squint is one that is detected only under conditions of stress, fatigue, illness, or clinical examination. It is revealed by use of the alternate cover test.

Amblyopia refers to a condition of poor vision in which the eye itself is healthy, but because of a refractive error, a difference in refraction between the two eyes, a squint, or opacities in the refractive media, the brain has either suppressed or has failed to develop the ability to perceive a detailed image from that eye. It is usually unilateral but may be bilateral in some circumstances, e.g. meridional amblyopia due to unrecognized astigmatism[146-8].

Assessment of visual acuity in infancy

The measurement of visual acuity in children under the age of three years is very difficult[149-52]. Various tests can be used to demonstrate that the child has reached a developmental stage at which visual fixation and concentration on tiny objects is possible. Examples include Sheridan's graded balls, the matching toys test, or the use of tiny sweets, known as hundreds and thousands (1 mm diameter). These tests provide an indication of visual function but cannot offer any measurement of visual acuity or any direct or indirect indication of refractive error.

An orthoptist can observe whether the eyes work together as a pair and can test the ability of each eye to take up fixation. Although no direct measurement of visual acuity can be made in infancy, inferences can be drawn about the likelihood of significantly impaired vision in either or both eyes. The orthoptic examination requires a high level of training and skill.

Several **new techniques** for the assessment of vision in infancy and early childhood are currently being investigated, e.g. forced choice preferential looking, and automated and semi-automated methods of detecting refractive error. None of these has yet reached the level of development where it could be recommended for the universal screening of infants[153-9].

We concluded that there is currently no satisfactory test of visual acuity suitable for the universal screening of children too young to co-operate with letter tests.

Visual acuity in pre-school children

Between the ages of two and three years, children become more able to co-operate with vision testing. It is usual to test distance vision at 6 m distance, in order to detect amblyopia, myopia, and astigmatism. Testing at 3 m is not recommended. A mirror is sometimes used if the testing room is less than 6 m long.

The visual acuity for distance vision can be assessed using either single letters (the Stycar test or preferably the Sheridan Gardiner cards) or a Snellen chart. Any of these can be used with a letter-matching card or with plastic letters so that the child does not have to be able to name the letters. A Snellen chart is preferable to single optotypes because the latter may seriously underestimate amblyopia or even miss the diagnosis altogether[160].

It is essential to occlude each eye in turn, otherwise the result indicates only the vision in the better eye. Around 67 per cent of children can tolerate occlusion at three years of age, but the figure rises to 80 per cent by 42 months[161].

Although it is the practice of most districts and health boards to recommend a visual acuity test for pre-school children, there is no clear evidence that screening for defects at this age results in a better outcome than diagnosis at school entry[163]. The poor performance of pre-school vision screening programmes is illustrated by their frequent failure to detect amblyopia until five or six years of age. Available tests are unsatisfactory—better tests are needed.

If the child can only read letter size 6/12 or less on the Snellen chart, in spite of good co-operation, referral is advisable. The referral criterion is 6/9 when single optotypes are used, provided that co-operation is satisfactory. The child should also be referred if there is a difference between the two eyes of two lines or more.

The routine testing of near vision seems to add very little to the detection of significant visual defects. Children with hypermetropia do not necessarily have a significant reduction of near visual acuity. Near vision testing can safely be omitted from the vision screening of children, although it does of course have a place in the assessment of the child with a suspected visual problem.

Myopia becomes increasingly common during the school years and a vision test every two or three years is therefore advisable.

Squint

The majority of manifest squints are first recognized by parents or relatives[163]. The parents should always be asked whether they have noticed any squint, laziness, or turning of one eye. Some parents are incorrectly informed that squint is normal under the age of six months and this can lead to delay in diagnosis of serious eye disease. A family history of high refractive error or squint in a first degree relative, may be significant and may justify referral for more detailed examination.

A careful inspection of the eyes should be made to identify any squint that has been overlooked or ignored by the child's parents. Some squints are not instantly apparent to simple inspection. In order to demonstrate these, the following tests may be used: the corneal reflections test; the cover test; the prism test; examination of eye movements by moving a small target of visual interest (not a light) through the horizontal, vertical, and oblique planes. Some or all of these procedures are widely used for screening, but the skill required for their proper performance and interpretation is not generally appreciated.

A common difficulty is the distinction between squint and pseudosquint (i.e. the appearance of squint caused by epicanthic folds). Squint and prominent epicanthic folds may co-exist.

Pseudosquint is the commonest single reason for referral to children's eye clinics.

Screening for latent squint involves the use of the alternate cover test. It is doubtful whether the detection of a latent squint before it becomes a problem clinically is of any significant benefit to the child.

We considered whether other health professionals should learn the techniques used by orthoptists, so that all infants and children could be screened in this way. Experienced clinicians commented on the considerable skill required and the need for proper training by an orthoptist.

Amblyopia

At present amblyopia is rarely diagnosed before the age of three years. By this time, visual acuity may be substantially reduced. The treatment of established amblyopia is not entirely satisfactory; although worthwhile gains in visual acuity can be achieved, they are not always maintained, nor can the development of good binocular vision be guaranteed. Amblyopia is a significant impairment because it prevents entry to certain careers and means that loss of the other 'good' eye results in serious disability[148].

The eventual goal of vision screening in children should be the *prevention* of amblyopia, by detection and treatment in infancy of the antecedent causes, in particular squint and anisometropia[164,165]. Although the latter could be detected by retinoscopy, the technique is not suitable for universal screening.

Orthoptist screening programmes

Universal screening by an orthoptist of all infants and children would result in detection of some vision defects that otherwise would be missed. The yield would probably be very small and would not justify this use of an orthoptist's expertise. A community-based orthoptist may, however, make a valuable contribution to secondary screening by examining children referred by parents or by other professional staff and selecting those who require a more detailed assessment. By this means, unnecessary referrals to a consultant ophthalmology clinic can be greatly reduced.

There is an increased incidence of visual defects in children with other serious neurological disabilities, and such children should undergo a specialist eye examination[166].

Screening techniques for the detection of refractive error in infancy are being developed (see p.51). Even if satisfactory sensitivity, specificity, and costing can be achieved, more research will be needed to determine whether very early treatment does in fact prevent amblyopia. We anticipate that these goals will eventually be reached and that the whole question of vision screening in children will then need to be re-examined.

Recommendations

We recommend that screening for visual defects in pre-school children should be confined to history and observation. Children with suspected defects, a significant family history or a neurological disorder should be examined by someone competent to give a definitive opinion.

We do not think there is conclusive evidence to support a more extensive screening programme for pre-school children. The question of visual acuity testing at age three to four years is discussed below. Staff who wish to carry out screening examinations for squint and other visual defects in pre-school children must first receive adequate instruction from an orthoptist.

A visual acuity test should be carried out at school entry.

Referral criteria should be as specified on p. 52. Children with a vision of 6/9 and those with a family history of myopia should be checked annually. With the above exceptions, children should have a further distance vision test at three-yearly intervals, i.e. aged 5, 8, 11, and 14, as myopia may appear at any age.

One person in each district should take responsibility for monitoring the results of vision screening.

Further research

There are several important areas for research. Research is continuing on the development and evaluation of vision in infancy, with the eventual aim of *preventing* amblyopia (see p. 54). Further work is needed to determine sensitivity, specificity and yield of a screening examination performed by staff other than orthoptists. We need a better pre-school acuity test.

It has been assumed by many authorities that the diagnosis of a minor vision defect at the age of three is preferable to diagnosis two years later at school entry, but further research is needed to determine whether this is in fact the case. Even if there is no proven benefit from earlier diagnosis in terms of better outcome, there is the practical advantage that the child starts school with the vision defect already diagnosed and corrected.

Districts and health boards who plan to continue with a test of visual acuity for pre-school children should ensure that the test is properly performed and that the results are evaluated[167]. Since some districts and boards will continue with a pre-school vision test, whereas others have already abandoned it, an ideal opportunity exists to make comparisons in such outcomes as success in treatment of amblyopia, accuracy of screening etc.

Any project to evaluate vision screening should include the following guidelines: a Snellen chart should be used if possible, resorting to single optotypes only when necessary. The vision must be checked in each eye separately. The test should be carried out at six metres distance in a properly illuminated room.

Visual acuity testing often presents practical difficulties in schools and there is undoubtedly scope for the development of new approaches. The value of testing all secondary school children for visual acuity defects at age 14 has been questioned. It is said that adolescents are unlikely to wear spectacles unless they themselves recognize a visual difficulty. The alternative approach might be self-referral, encouraged by the inclusion of eye care as a topic in health education curricula.

Colour vision defects

Deficiencies in colour discrimination, primarily affecting the perception of reds and greens, occur in 8 per cent of boys and in about 0.5 per cent of girls[168]. Blue deficiencies and total colour blindness are extremely rare.

Two reasons are advanced for the early detection of colour vision defects. First, it has been suggested that they might cause learning difficulties, particularly with regard to colour coded materials used in the teaching of reading and maths[169,170]. There is in fact little evidence that colour vision defects do cause learning difficulties and most affected children can distinguish different colour materials in spite of reduced colour discrimination. Second, colour vision defects preclude people from entering certain careers and it is helpful for a person to know that they have this deficiency at an early stage in career planning.

Screening at the beginning of secondary schooling might be useful, by providing information that would be important in career selection. The Ishihara test appears to have the most satisfactory performance, although it is very sensitive and detects even very minor defects. The City University test is preferred by some.

Recommendations

No attempt should be made to screen for colour vision defects in primary school, but a test should be offered to all 11-year-olds. A case could be made for including only boys, in view of the much higher incidence; but as the test is so quick and simple at this age, it is probably justifiable to test both boys and girls.

Children found to have a colour vision defect should be told that they have a difficulty in discriminating colours which *might* be important with regard to certain career choices. In cases where the defect may have important career implications, expert advice should be obtained from an ophthalmologist and/or a careers adviser.

Research needs

It is not known whether children value and make use of the discovery of a colour vision defect. An alternative approach which has been suggested is to include eye care and colour vision defects in a health education lesson. Children who felt that such defects might be relevant to their career plans would be invited to attend for a screening test. There is still uncertainty about the most appropriate test, referral criteria, and action to be taken when a defect is found.

Summary of recommendations on vision screening

1. An active approach to the early detection of disabling vision defects in infancy should be pursued, making use of the various methods outlined on p. 49.
2. Parents should be encouraged to report any concerns regarding their child's vision. Specific questions should be asked about family history, visual function, and squint.
3. An inspection of the eyes to detect squint should be part of any paediatric examination. Fundoscopy should be undertaken where there is a clinical indication.
4. A test of visual acuity should be performed at school entry, and at three-year intervals thereafter.
5. A colour vision screening test should be carried out between the ages of nine and thirteen.

10

Screening for hearing impairment

Types of hearing impairment

Hearing impairment is of two main types:

1. Sensorineural hearing loss (SNHL) is caused by a lesion in the cochlea or the auditory nerve and its central connections. It may be unilateral or bilateral. Important causes include intra-uterine infections, dysmorphic syndromes, severe jaundice, meningitis, and genetic causes[171].
2. Conductive hearing loss is related to middle ear pathology[172,173]. In developed countries this is usually due to secretory otitis media (SOM).* In poorer communities, there may be chronic suppurative otitis media with discharge and perforation. Very rarely there is a malformation of the middle ear. SNHL and middle ear disease may coexist.

Incidence of hearing impairment

Significant bilateral SNHL occurs in between one and two births per thousand[174]. The incidence is higher in babies admitted to neonatal intensive care units. Conductive hearing loss is extremely common. At least a quarter of pre-school children have one or more episodes of SOM, and it may be found in 5–10 per cent of children over the age of five at some time in the early school years. A much smaller number of children have severe persistent SOM.

---

* Also called 'Otitis media with effusion'.

Effects and management of hearing impairment

In the absence of appropriate intervention most children with SNHL will suffer serious impairment of language acquisition. Intervention with amplification and appropriate teaching help the child to acquire a means of communication either by speech, signing, or both[175,176]. Although there is no proof that very early diagnosis improves the outcome, there are good theoretical reasons for expecting this to be the case[177].

The extent of the disability caused by SOM is more controversial. In children with no other adverse factors it probably has a minimal influence on speech and language development. Severe persistent SOM may however result in significant delay in language acquisition and also in behaviour disturbance, particularly in children with other disabilities[178,179].

Some children are at particular risk of developing severe SOM. This group of children includes those with Down's syndrome, cleft palate, Turner's syndrome, and facial malformation syndromes. A more aggressive approach to surgical treatment may be beneficial in these children[180].

Surgery is effective in the short-term, but the long-term benefits are much less certain[181]. For the majority of children who are not severely affected, conservative management is advocated by many authorities. Decongestants are rarely effective but antibiotic therapy may help. An alternative approach for the most severely affected children is provision of a low-power hearing aid; continued audiological and educational supervision is essential.

Simply explaining the nature of the problem to parents or teachers is often helpful. Once they understand that the child has a hearing loss, they can communicate more effectively. A copy of the child's test results, or audiogram, with appropriate explanation, is reassuring.

Detection of hearing impairment

Parents sometimes recognize severe hearing loss themselves, but hearing loss of moderate degree, or predominantly affecting high frequencies, is easily overlooked, sometimes for several years[182]. A good case can therefore be made for screening.

Since most cases of significant SNHL are congenital and the process of language acquisition begins at birth, the obvious time to screen is in the neonatal period. Neonatal screening would not detect all children with hearing loss and it might still be necessary to carry out a further screening test, because:

1. SNHL due to congenital rubella and cytomegalovirus may deteriorate during the first two years of life, even though not readily detectable in the neonatal period.
2. Some types of genetically determined SNHL are progressive and may present at any time in childhood.
3. SOM may be acquired at any time during childhood.

Screening—birth to six months

Screening for hearing loss may be undertaken by a number of methods[183-6]:

1. Universal neonatal screening, using: (a) an automated behavioural method, the auditory response cradle (ARC); (b) brain-stem evoked response audiometry (BSERA), an objective method involving recording and computer analysis of EEG signals evoked in response to a series of clicks; and (c) measurement of cochlear emissions, a promising research technique which also requires a sophisticated electronic measuring and analysis system. The relative merits of screening infants by ARC, BSERA, or cochlear emission tests are still being debated and the choice depends to some extent on local preference and facilities.

Universal neonatal screening, although expensive, is attractive because it offers access to a 'captive population'. Improved organizational procedures are needed to ensure that all infants are tested, including those discharged from hospital early or born at home[187].

2. Selective neonatal screening of high risk-groups, for example infants requiring intensive care or exchange transfusion,

infants with congenital infection or dysmorphic syndromes, and those with a family history of hearing loss. Case finding may be achieved via neonatal intensive care units, post-natal wards, and the primary care team.

3. Making use of parental observations. These can be enhanced by the use of a check-list that alerts parents to the existence of hearing loss in babies and tells them what to look for[188].

Distraction test

Behavioural testing during the first year of life involves a technique known as the distraction test. This requires two people working in collaboration[189-91]. It depends on the infant's ability to turn and localize a sound source. A developmental maturity level of around seven months is optimum for this test. Prior to this age, sitting balance, head control, and sound localization ability are imperfect. Beyond ten months of age, the development of object permanence and increasing sociability make the test more difficult.

Quiet conditions, adequate sound level monitoring, and careful technique are essential. Although the distraction technique can be applied at any age, it is ideally suited for testing children around six to nine months of age.

The few published studies on the performance of this screening procedure under field conditions are not encouraging[192], but good results *can* be obtained[193]. We think therefore that the distraction screening test should be continued. The following conditions must be fulfilled:

(1) technique must be meticulous and the standard guidelines must be observed;

(2) adequate testing conditions must be provided;

(3) clear referral instructions relevant to local circumstances must be devised and adhered to;

(4) a diagnostic and support service must be available to see referrals promptly.

When inadequately performed the distraction screening test is not merely valueless but is positively harmful, because the child's apparent responses to sound may persuade parents that their own worries about the child's hearing were unfounded. This can lead to long delays in diagnosis.

Hearing tests—eighteen months to five years

Between the ages of 18 and 42 months, it becomes possible to test hearing by methods involving co-operation. Speech discrimination tasks require the child to respond by pointing to a series of objects named by the examiner in a very quiet voice. These tests are enjoyed by children and are easily learnt and applied accurately. Examples include the McCormick Toy Test[191] and the Kendal Test. Most children can perform these successfully by 39 months of age. At or beyond this age, inability to co-operate with the Toy Test is suggestive either of a hearing difficulty or some more general developmental problem.

The child may alternatively be required to give some behavioural response to measured sound, produced either by voice or by a free field warbler or audiometer. These so-called performance tests are particularly useful when testing children whose first language is not English and no staff are available who speak the child's own language.

For the more mature and co-operative child, the free field audiometer can be replaced by the standard pure-tone audiometer with headphones. Pure tone audiometry is often seen as the 'standard' by which other methods are assessed, although it can be argued that the ability to discriminate speech in everyday surroundings is just as important.

Screening pre-school children

We considered whether any further pre-school screening test of hearing should be undertaken after the age of ten months. The argument in favour of a further test is that a few children with acquired or progressive SNHL and those with severe SOM may otherwise elude diagnosis, with possibly serious consequences for their education.

The disadvantages of such a policy would be: (a) the low yield of important new positive findings; (b) the high incidence of SOM; and (c) the difficulty of determining which cases of SOM are transient and which are persistent.

We concluded that no attempt should be made to undertake a universal screening test of hearing after the age of seven to nine months, until the child goes to school. An audiological assessment should be arranged for any child who has: (a) significantly impaired language development; (b) a history of chronic or repeated middle ear disease or upper airway obstruction; or (c) developmental or behavioural problems.

Testing at school entry

The school entry 'sweep' test of hearing consists of a modified pure tone audiogram performed at fixed intensity level[194,195]. Criteria for failure on this test vary from 20dB through 25–30dB at one or more frequencies and after one or two tests[196].

Many variables affect the results of this procedure, including ambient noise, the skill of the screener, and the maturity of the child.

The school entry 'sweep' test should be continued, but its limitations are recognized and further research is needed. Although very few cases of SNHL remain undiagnosed at this age, SOM is very common, and may have educational implications even if treatment is not thought to be necessary in many cases. Since the referral criteria and management of SOM remain controversial and treatment resources are overstretched, each district and health board should define precisely its own policy and monitor the results[14].

Further screening tests of hearing after school entry appear to have a very small yield and we do not think they can be justified. However, a hearing test should be undertaken on any child experiencing learning or behavioural difficulties.

Impedance measurement is a technique for assessing middle ear function and therefore of detecting fluid in the middle ear[172,173]. It does not give a direct measure of hearing levels. It is a very sensitive test, which detects even minor degrees of middle ear dysfunction. At present, it is reserved for use as a diagnostic procedure in specialist clinics, but it may offer an alternative approach to screening for SOM.

Better monitoring is needed

We found that districts and health boards vary widely in the number of tests carried out, their referral policy, and in the ease of access to treatment. Surprisingly few districts or health boards can provide data on the effectiveness of their programme. There is therefore very little firm evidence on which to base our recommendations and it is clear that better monitoring at district or health board level and further basic research are needed.

Recommendations

Our recommendations are as follows:

1. Neonatal screening, whether selective or universal, is a promising approach but should at present be regarded as a research procedure.

2. A systematic approach to increasing parental awareness about hearing loss should be adopted, such as the use of a check-list.

3. Parental suspicions about possible hearing loss must be taken seriously and a rapid efficient referral route to an audiological centre must be available in *every* part of the country. No parent who expresses concern about a child's hearing should be denied prompt referral to the audiological service.

4. The distraction test of hearing should be continued but it is essential that the standard of testing and the results are monitored critically and kept under review.

5. Whenever a pre-school child is seen, it should be routine to ask the parents whether they have any concerns about the child's hearing. Parental concern is a sufficient indication for diagnostic testing.

6. No universal screening test of hearing is recommended between the first birthday and school entry, but any child whose hearing is in doubt must be referred for diagnostic testing.

7. Children with conditions which put them at high risk of middle ear disease should be tested at regular intervals in a clinic with full diagnostic facilities, including impedance equipment.

8. The school entry sweep test of hearing should be continued. No further routine test of hearing is recommended.

9. Impedence testing is not recommended for screening at present, but merits further research.

10. Audiological assessment and follow-up should be arranged for any young child who has had bacterial meningitis or prolonged treatment with ototoxic drugs, either before or soon after discharge from hospital.

11. It is important that health authorities provide adequate conditions for hearing testing and that the staff involved have their own hearing tested every two years.

12. All staff involved with screening tests of hearing should have access to a sound level meter, and proper training in its use.

13. Screening is of *no* value unless *comprehensive* audiological diagnostic and treatment facilities are available. All parents with hearing impaired children should have access to a centre with such facilities, and the need for paediatric, psychological, and genetic advice must also be met.

14. One person in each district or health board should take responsibility for co-ordinating the programme of hearing screening, including training and refresher courses. Information should be collected on the coverage of screening pro-

grammes, the number of referrals, delays experienced between referral and diagnosis and between diagnosis and treatment, and the average age at which SNHL is diagnosed.

Research needs

Research is needed on many aspects of screening for hearing loss, including techniques, organization, and yield. For example, What is the most cost effective approach to neonatal screening? Does treatment improve the outcome of SOM sufficiently to justify screening? How should the results of the distraction test and the sweep test be monitored and how can high standards of testing be maintained? What is the rôle of impedance testing in the screening of school entrants?

11

Screening for developmental impairments

One of the aims of child health surveillance is to identify children whose development is abnormally slow or is following a deviant path. The impairment may involve motor, intellectual, language, or emotional development. The resulting disability may range from trivial to profound and a wide variety of underlying disorders may be responsible.

Examples of impairments that are likely to result in *serious* and usually *permanent* disability include:

(1) cerebral palsy;
(2) muscular dystrophy and other muscle diseases;
(3) mental retardation (severe learning difficulties);
(4) specific speech and language disorders, including the rare childhood dysphasias;
(5) autism.

There are also a number of impairments that cause significant disability in early childhood and are likely to affect educational progress, but tend to improve as the child matures. Such impairments are sometimes described as *'developmental'*. Examples include:

1. Borderline or mild global backwardness (mild learning difficulties, developmental delay).
2. Delay in speech and language acquisition.
3. Clumsiness.
4. Specific learning disabilities (defined as a difficulty in mastering individual skills such as reading, not explicable by sensory defects, low IQ or inadequate teaching).

Definitions

Impairments may be detected by a variety of means, one of which is developmental examination. The terms developmental examination and developmental screening are defined and discussed in the following paragraphs.

Developmental examination is a clinical procedure designed to evaluate the level of development reached by a child at a particular point in time, and to detect any significant deviations from the normal. It usually includes an interview with the parents, structured observations, and the administration of specific tasks or tests. The developmental examination may be undertaken as a screening procedure[26,197,198] or as part of the assessment of a suspected problem.

Interpretation of a developmental examination relies on a comparison of the abilities of the child being examined with those of other children of the same age. The data about normal development needed to make this comparison are available in various developmental tests, charts, and scales.

Developmental tests and scales vary in the extent to which they take account of parents' views. Although parents cannot always recall past milestones accurately, they are an excellent source of information about current performance. Furthermore, it is essential to understand and respect the way in which the parents perceive their child and any difficulties in development, before constructive discussion and planning can take place[199-201].

The term 'developmental screening' refers to the performance of one or more developmental examinations *on every child* at specified key ages in infancy and early childhood. As with other screening tests, the aim is to examine *all* apparently normal children in order to identify those who may have some undetected abnormality.

Developmental tests

Several developmental screening tests[202-12] are available. The Denver Developmental Screening Test (DDST) and the Woodside Test are the two most popular tests and adequate data are available to examine their effectiveness. In addition, a number of tests have been devised with the aim of recognizing speech and language disorders at an early stage, for example Egan's 'bus puzzle' test. All these tests have two important characteristics: simple, standardized test items and clearly defined pass/fail rules for referral.

Because of this rigid structure, many professionals distrust standardized screening tests. The alternative approach is to base routine developmental examinations on a broad knowledge of child development, supported where necessary by one of the popular developmental scales. This approach requires greater flexibility and allows for the exercise of professional judgement.

Screening, assessment, and surveillance

For reasons to be discussed below, we do not think any of the methods of developmental screening can meet the requirements for a screening test laid down by Cochrane and Holland (p. 9).

Failure of developmental screening to meet these criteria has been recognized for some years. Many authorities have argued that each routine developmental examination should be regarded as an assessment rather than a screening test[213]. It is nevertheless claimed that regular examinations of apparently normal children, although not fulfilling the strict criteria for a screening test, have two important functions:

1. They facilitate the detection of various impairments affecting development.

2. They provide an opportunity to discuss child development with the parents and to reassure them that the child is developing normally.

We had considerable difficulty in evaluating the role and value of routine developmental examination for three reasons. First, there are several developmental tests and scales in widespread use, and there is immense variation in the skill and the manner in which they are used. Second, the purpose of the developmental examination is to detect not just one, but many different conditions affecting development. Finally, the need for and value of advice and reassurance is difficult to measure and evaluate.

In this section we will discuss the following questions.

1. Is there a place for routine developmental examination in detecting:
   (a) serious impairments as defined on p. 68?
   (b) the impairments we have labelled 'developmental', as listed on p. 68?
   (c) speech and language delay?
   (d) educational problems in school entrants?

2. How effective is developmental examination as a means of involving, educating and reassuring parents about aspects of child development and rearing?

Detection of serious impairments

The working party examined first the need for routine developmental examinations as a means of detecting serious impairments[214]. These conditions, although individually rare, have serious effects on the individual child and collectively form a significant health burden for society. The incidence of these conditions is as follows: cerebral palsy, 0.15–0.3 per cent (1.5–3 cases per 1000); Duchenne muscular dystrophy, 0.03 per cent of males (3 per 10 000 male births); severe learning difficulties, 0.37 per cent (3.7 cases per thousand); specific language disorders (no accurate data available); autism, 0.03 per cent (3 cases per 10 000 births).

These disorders are rarely amenable to treatment in the medical sense, but much can be done to prevent secondary handicap, and the early detection of these disorders is believed to be worthwhile for the reasons mentioned previously (Chapter 3).

Diagnosis of these conditions in infancy is notoriously difficult and serious mistakes are easily made[215]. Routine developmental examinations inevitably lead to referrals of doubtful cases, but even the most experienced may be unable to establish for certain whether a child will have a significant disability. In most cases, diagnosis rests on clinical judgement and the evolution of the problem over time, since there is rarely any reference test or investigation available to confirm or refute the diagnosis of a serious impairment.

Although routine developmental examinations are capable of detecting extreme deviations from normal development[216, 217], most serious impairments are found by other means[45] (Chapter 4), and there seems to be little need for a programme of developmental screening to detect them.

Since inappropriate reassurance of parents by professionals continues to be a common cause of delay in diagnosis[41,182], all health care workers should be aware of the conditions listed above and should respond appropriately to parental concerns. Paediatricians must ensure that children who are at risk of neurological defects for any reason receive expert follow-up.

Detection of developmental disorders

We looked next at the place of routine developmental examinations in detecting children with developmental impairments such as those listed on p. 68. A number of fundamental difficulties were identified. These centred around:

1. The difficulty of defining who should be regarded as a 'patient' or 'case'.
2. The unpredictable natural history of developmental impairments in early childhood.
3. The lack of clear evidence as to when intervention is appropriate or effective.

It is not possible to give precise incidence or prevalence figures for these conditions because they cannot be defined exactly. There is no absolute distinction between, for example, normal and abnormal speech[218-22], or between excessive clumsiness[223] and acceptable motor competence.

Children do not all develop at the same rate, nor do they all follow the same sequence of development[224,225]. They may show substantial discrepancies in the rate of progress in various aspects of development: between for example motor and speech development. Children whose rate of develoment is so slow as to place them in the slowest 3 per cent of the population have an increased risk of significant and persistent problems, but nevertheless many eventually are found to be normal. For example, some of the children who walk late (i.e. later than 18 months) have a neurological disorder or are mentally handicapped, but the majority when examined a few years later are found to be normal and reveal no significant motor or intellectual impairment. Conversely, children with significant abnormalities such as hemiplegia may achieve their developmental milestones well within the so-called normal range.

This means that the developmental examination is in itself seldom diagnostic. There is no precise age at which failure to achieve a certain milestone can be said to be abnormal. Whatever cut-off point may be selected for screening purposes, many normal children will fail the test while some with significant problems will pass.

Referral criteria

The decision to refer a child for more detailed evaluation depends not only on the result of a screening test but also on whether the parents themselves consider the child to have a problem affecting development. This in turn is dependent, at least in part, on their education, social status, and expectations for their children[226-9].

We could find no clear-cut criteria for identifying those children who might benefit most from early assessment and intervention. It is possible that the extent to which opportunities for play and learning are available in the child's home might be a more relevant criterion when considering the need for early intervention, rather than the actual level of the developmental attainment[230].

Speech and language problems

Delays in the acquisition of speech and language require special consideration: they are common, they can be the presenting feature of other serious disorders, and severely impaired children start school at a disadvantage and many of them still have significant verbal deficits by secondary school age[231-9]. The extent to which these problems can be alleviated by early intensive intervention requires further research[240], but nevertheless these children have a right to the most appropriate educational support currently available.

Because of the very wide variations in the rate of normal language acquisition it is extremely difficult to detect those children who will need additional help, until they reach the age of about three years. Similarly, there is at present no simple screening procedure capable of distinguishing between the large number of 'late normal' children and the few who suffer from the various rare childhood dysphasias and language disorders.

Early intervention

The working party examined the evidence in favour of early educational intervention for children with delayed or impaired development[241-6]. Children living in conditions of extreme adversity are able to make substantial progress if their quality of care and stimulation is improved. Such gains can be accomplished at least as late as eight or nine years. However, early education is potentially beneficial for *all* children and not just those who are slow. Indeed, advantaged children probably gain *more* from such facilities[247-55]. The effects are dependent on the quality of the intervention and particularly on the involvement of the parents. Although substantial increases in measured intelligence are seldom achieved, improvements can be shown to occur in attitudes, attendance records etc., even many years later. There is less literature on interventions such as speech therapy[240]; it seems likely that the same principles apply and there is a little evidence that programmes which involve parents may be more successful.

Health professionals and parents may believe that decisions about referral criteria following developmental checks are based on medical and scientific considerations. There is however good reason to think that the most important factor governing decision-making is the availability of and ease of access to diagnostic and remedial services[254].

School entrant examinations

A developmental examination at school entry (five years of age) to detect potential learning difficulties, clumsiness, and specific learning disabilities, is recommended by some authorities[256-61]. The examination idea has been criticized because it includes a number of unstable 'soft' neurological signs, is unstandardized[223], and like other screening procedures in education does not distinguish sufficiently precisely between children who will progress normally and those who will eventually require extra help.

Continuous monitoring of a child's progress should be an intrinsic part of the teacher's role, enabling the curriculum, content, and process of teaching to be modified for each child's individual needs[262-5].

Developmental guidance

We considered next the role of routine developmental examinations in helping, advising, and reassuring parents. Fundamental to this idea is the belief that parents need, want, and value such help, and that without regular professional support and supervision parents might not be capable of recognizing abnormal development or of taking appropriate action. It is this belief that gave rise to the term 'surveillance'.

There are many parents who need professional assistance of various kinds in bringing up their children. Some have difficulties with basic child-rearing skills. Others fail to recognize the signs of disease or disability, or are too distressed to seek the help their child needs (see p. 16). Such parents can be helped by a programme of child health surveillance, both in identifying the problem and in obtaining appropriate intervention.

However, the majority of parents now expect a different kind of relationship with their professional advisers. They want to be involved in decisions regarding their children's developmental problems and they do not necessarily benefit from a purely medical approach, which perceives developmental delays and impairments as a form of pathology that requires treatment. They nevertheless value guidance on how to handle such difficulties in the most constructive way possible, while avoiding the use of stigmatizing medical labels.

The main role of the primary health care professional in most families will be to provide expert knowledge where it is needed, in order to help parents to understand child development more effectively and to participate in decisions affecting the child's management. This does not necessarily imply that families must be seen on a one-to-one basis; more radical and imaginative approaches have been advocated in order to involve the parents more actively and extend not only their knowledge of child development but also advance their attitudes to learning. Interventions that involve parents in this way may bring about worthwhile long-term changes[249,263].

Developmental examination is also believed by some authorities to provide an effective vehicle for defining a child's educational needs to both parent and teacher at school entry. We could not find any evidence of the extent to which the information acquired through these examinations is utilized or valued by teachers. We concluded, as did the British Paediatric Association Report on the school health service, that there is no justification for a detailed developmental examination of all school entrants on a *routine* basis[266,267].

Conclusions

We conclude that the routine developmental examination of *all* children as a means of detecting impairments is unnecessary in the case of serious disorders such as cerebral palsy and severe learning difficulties, and we doubt its relevance to the detection of developmental impairments such as delayed language acquisition.

We believe that the problems we encountered are intrinsic to the whole concept of detecting defects by routine developmental examinations using standardized screening tests. They would not be solved by devising different tests. A more efficient and effective way to facilitate early detection of problems affecting development is to ensure that staff have a detailed knowledge of child development and an awareness of the various impairments which may affect it.

All children should be included in the programme of child health surveillance and screening. Opportunities to evaluate development are available when the child is seen for the screening procedures that we have specified; whenever the child is seen for any other reason; and on alternative or additional occasions as dictated by circumstances. The need for a detailed developmental examination on each occasion should be a matter of professional judgement.

Recommendations

There is no justification for repeated developmental examinations on a routine basis of all pre-school or school children and these should be discontinued.

Parents' concerns must be taken seriously. No parent who is worried about any aspect of their child's development should be denied access to the appropriate professional for expert assessment. Similarly, teachers should have easy access to professional advice for health problems affecting their pupils.

Formal tests and rigid rules regarding indications for referral are undesirable. Instead, we stress that staff must be able to: (a) listen carefully to parents' worries; (b) take a proper developmental history; (c) observe accurately; (d) recognize atypical patterns of development; and (e) make appropriate referral recommendations.

We do not think there is any need for detailed developmental charts to be maintained for each child. Such charts perpetuate the 'pass/fail' concept of screening.

All staff require a thorough knowledge of child development. Developmental tests, charts, and scales should be regarded as an aid to the acquisition and application of this knowledge (see page 69).

Professional judgement, in the light of local policy and the needs and wishes of parents, should be exercised in deciding how much time should be spent reviewing each child's development.

Health professionals must work closely with their colleagues in the field of education to ensure that children with special needs receive the services to which they are entitled under the 1981 Education Act.

A new approach?

The working party believes that the approach to developmental surveillance outlined here has a number of advantages:

1. It emphasizes the important role of *parents* both in detecting and in acknowledging the possibility of developmental problems.
2. It recognizes the reality that in a large majority of children, *adequately trained* professionals can satisfy themselves that the child's development is within normal limits, without undertaking a detailed developmental examination.
3. It lays greater emphasis on the role of the *developmental history* and on *observation*.
4. It acknowledges that individuals working in different parts of the country will be familiar with a particular structure of

developmental examination; we do not think it is either realistic or necessary to recommend a single format of developmental test to be used universally.

5. By eliminating detailed developmental examinations in cases where they are clearly not necessary, more professional time is released which can be spent with those parents and children who need expert help and support but at present do not always receive it.

Research required

Research opportunities in child development and intervention are extensive but there are exceptional methodological difficulties. Collaboration between health and educational professionals is essential. Examples of questions which deserve study are:

1. How can we monitor our success in achieving the aims of early detection and appropriate intervention?
2. What are the best ways of involving parents in an increasing understanding of children's needs?
3. Which children are most likely to benefit from specialized educational programmes, in particular those devised for pre-school children with speech and language difficulties?
4. What is the role of health professionals in educational counselling and assessment?
5. The lack of data regarding the incidence of serious language disorders is related to the inadequacy of current definitions. Further research on the characterization of these conditions is needed[236].
6. Our recommendations include a need for substantial improvements in both quality and quantity of training, but little is known about the best material or methods for providing this, nor about the implications for personnel and facilities (see Chapter 16).

12

Screening for psychiatric disorders

Psychiatric and social problems are very common in childhood[268,269]. Examples include pre-school adjustment disorder, neurotic and conduct disorders, eating disorders such as anorexia nervosa in the adolescent and pre-adolescent child, psychosocial growth failure, child abuse, etc. Associated problems include parental psychiatric disorders, marital disharmony, and poor living conditions. The working party did not have the expertise to undertake a detailed review of surveillance for all these psychiatric disorders.

Pre-school adjustment disorders are of particular importance, and include disturbances of behaviour such as overactivity, poor impulse control, excessive aggression, sleeping disturbances, and conflicts over appetite and eating. Seven per cent of three-year-olds are said to show moderate or severe adjustment problems. In up to two-thirds of cases behavioural disturbance may still be noted at eight years of age[270-2]. Although individual case studies confirm that treatment may be effective, there are no large-scale population studies to demonstrate the feasibility of providing effective intervention programmes for whole communities.

Screening by check-list

It is possible to carry out screening using check-lists, such as the behaviour check-list or the behaviour screening questionnaire[273]. The use of a screening test helps to highlight problems and may enable parents to recognize that their child does exhibit a significant behaviour disturbance. There are close parallels between screening for psychiatric disorder and developmental screening. Decisions about referral depend on discussion with the parents, their perceptions of disorder, their willingness to make use of psychiatric or psychological help and the availability of such services.

Recommendations

Staff should be aware of the high incidence of behaviour problems in young children and should enquire routinely about any difficulties with behaviour and management. Training is needed to inform staff about the common behaviour problems. They must also be familiar with the options available for treatment.

Behavioural screening questionnaires should not be used routinely, but they may be introduced in training programmes and used in selected cases under appropriate supervision. Adequate support and referral services are essential if staff are to develop the confidence to recognize cases that may benefit from expert treatment and to manage straightforward problems themselves[274-6].

Finally, psychiatric problems in school-age children and adolescents are often referred initially to the school medical service. There should be a greater emphasis on child psychiatry and psychology in training programmes for staff in the school health service.

13

Health education

Health education deserves greater commitment and more resources than it has received in the past. The members of the working party believe that too much emphasis has been placed on developmental surveillance as a means of discovering defects in children.

The philosophy of health promotion is particularly relevant to health education. The didactic approach commonly adopted by professionals is often ineffective and may alienate some parents. Changes of attitude and behaviour are more likely to be achieved by parents who have been helped to accept responsibility for their own and their child's health.

Is health education effective?

It is not easy to demonstrate the impact of health education campaigns, and the results of some research studies have been inconclusive or disappointing[277-80]. Few health education campaigns occur in isolation; they are usually commenced against an existing background of knowledge. This may explain why it is difficult to demonstrate substantial differences between a group subjected to an intensive education campaign and a control group. Nevertheless the combination of publicity campaigns and discussion with individuals does seem capable of bringing about changes in people's behaviour.

An important observation was made by the Scottish Health Education Unit:

It is impossible to separately quantify the contribution of health education elements within a total health programme. It is naive to equate effectiveness measures in therapy and prevention since there is typically a large time gap between uptake of preventive measures and the individual's exposure to risk . . . The index of effectiveness must be in terms of the community at large.

Accidents and accident prevention

Whether measured in terms of morbidity or mortality, accidents are among the most important problems in child health after the first year[281-90]. The type of accident that occurs relates to the developmental level a child has reached, and it is logical therefore to include accident prevention in training programmes on child development and developmental examination.

Community-based accident prevention programmes must of course involve not only health professionals but also many other disciplines. However, health professionals have two important roles: (i) to collect the data on accidents from which prevention programmes can be improved and evaluated; and (ii) to play a full part in the educational components of such programmes. The primary health care team should include accident prevention as an important component of its approach to health education.

Topics for health education

Examples of areas where health education may be beneficial include the following.

The *neonatal* and *six week* checks provide an opportunity to identify and discuss areas of possible concern such as parent–infant interaction, breast feeding, contraception, and sibling problems[291-3].

Both professionals and parents need continuing education on the value of *immunization*[1-3]. Uptake can be considerably increased if staff are committed to immunization and sound training is available regarding the indications and contra-indications for each individual immunization.

There is scope for health professionals to be involved in the *prevention of accidents and child abuse*. Examples include:

(1) ensuring that parents demand child-resistant containers for drugs and hazardous household chemicals;

(2) advising about child safety devices;

(3) advising about safe nursery furniture;

(4) drawing attention to potentially dangerous areas within the home (glass, stairs, windows, balconies) and in the garden (gates, pools, ponds);

(5) safe transport in cars;

(6) safety of toys, playgrounds, etc.;

(7) awareness of appropriate response to unwanted advances from strangers, self-protection against sexual abuse.

Education should be offered about the appropriate responses to minor ailments, such as diarrhoea and illnesses associated with high fever.

Advice about feeding practices, nutrition, vitamin supplements, etc. may be needed. Prevention of rickets should be emphasized in high-risk populations[294].

Guidance on development is beneficial: what to expect, how to promote learning, how to recognize developmental disorders. At the same time, the evolution and avoidance of behaviour problems can be explained[295,296].

Dental care is important; information should be provided about hygiene, the use of fluoride in appropriate cases, and regular dental inspections. The advice to be given should be planned in collaboration with local dental services[297-300].

Some parents need help in making use of available resources and services. For example, parents and children living in deprived circumstances and those whose first language is not English have difficulty in forming social contacts with other families.

It is important to recognize the factors which may predict an increased risk of *child abuse*, so that preventive intervention can be attempted. There is evidence that many of the risk factors for child abuse can be recognized in the pregnancy and in the first few days of the puerperium. Appropriate professional guidance, practical help, development of a supportive network involving family and friends, and increasing the parents' knowledge of child development may all help to reduce the incidence of child abuse[301-9].

Appropriate counselling of teenagers, including guidance on such matters as drugs and alcohol abuse, contraception, AIDS, physical exercise, diet, obesity, etc., may be welcomed in secondary schools. Caring for teenage mothers and their babies presents special problems[310-13].

It has been suggested that the incidence of sudden infant death syndrome (SIDS) can be reduced by appropriate health supervision[127-9].

Recommendations

We recommend that each district or health board should have a policy specifying which aspects of health education are to be emphasized and what is to be taught. They should support wholeheartedly all the initiatives currently aimed at increasing immunization uptake. Further, a more determined effort should be made to prevent accidents by all the means currently available and each district or health board should investigate ways of monitoring the success of this programme. For example, an audit of all serious accidents in the under-fives might be undertaken.

Research required

The content, effectiveness and delivery of health education and developmental guidance ('anticipatory guidance', in the USA literature) require much further study[214].

Accident prevention programmes vary widely in effectiveness. Research is needed on the reasons for the differences, methods of implementation, and ways of collecting data for monitoring purposes.

14

Records

Few districts or health boards would wish to change their present records system unless persuaded that there was a satisfactory nationally agreed alternative. The working party did not feel that it would be realistic at this stage to recommend any particular record card or book for the entire country.

We suggest that the possibility of a single record format should be explored. For example, it would be helpful if a universal size of record card could be agreed and it has been suggested that a national design for a record folder might be a practical proposition. Each record should have space for recording the results of the screening procedures we have described as the 'core programme'. The composition of the present working party was not appropriate for the task of designing records. We are pleased to record that **a newly constituted working party has been convened for this purpose,** and will report as soon as possible.

What are records for?

Records have to serve multiple purposes. These can be listed as follows:

1. Records contain personal identification data.
2. They provide a graphical record of physical growth.
3. They record information about normal and abnormal development, immunization, illnesses etc. which forms a basis for future professional decision-making.

4. The records may be used by parents as a basis for discussing problems of child development or education with professional advisors.

5. They may be required for legal purposes, for example to demonstrate that the health authority's programme of child care was in fact delivered, or it may need to be presented in court in support of care proceedings.

6. Records may be used as a summary of intended actions in respect of children with special needs. If held by parents it can be used by educational and social services as well as health care staff.

7. Records may be used in training and supervision of staff.

8. A record may be useful for research purposes. Retrospective analysis of such records is of limited value but they may be useful in planned prospective research.

9. Child health records also provide information for the monitoring of the surveillance programme and for the provision of Korner-compatible data.

It is very difficult for a single record to fulfil all these functions. On the other hand, any system that involves two separate records increases the amount of time involved in their maintenance and this is likely to result in reduced standards and incomplete information.

Parent-held records

There is an increasing weight of opinion that parents should hold the child's main record[314]. Recent legislation implies that parents will have an increasing right to examine their child's medical records, and parents are no more likely to lose the record than are professionals.

If held by parents, the record is available for consultation to any professional involved with the child. Further, parent-held records are in keeping with the philosophy that parents should be treated as equal partners in child health care.

We conclude that the parent-held record is a desirable development and one that should be supported. Nevertheless, we recognize the need for some information to be held by health professionals. This must include personal information, a note as to whether the agreed health surveillance checks and immunizations have been carried out, and if so the dates and the outcome. These details should be in a form in which they can readily be entered into a computer record system[315,316]. There must also be space for clinical notes, the names of people to whom referrals have been made and the outcome, and the information required for overall monitoring.

We are not enthusiastic about the idea of a detailed developmental record chart for each child. We would see this as a continuation of the 'box ticking' approach to developmental screening, which we believe to be outdated. In cases where a child's development gives cause for concern a developmental record may be very useful, but is likely to be more profitable when it forms part of an intervention programme.

15

Organization and service delivery

The aim of the child health service should be to ensure that *all* children are covered by the professional network, since children not known to any general practitioner, those who are socially mobile, and those who do not attend any child health clinics are likely to constitute high-risk groups. It is precisely these children who are most difficult to monitor. In areas of high social mobility such as the inner cities it is very difficult for any central register to be kept up to date even with a computerized system.

There is widespread and justified concern about the health needs of inner city children and their families, but it should be remembered that their problems are not unique; sparsely populated rural areas where there is high unemployment also present particular problems of service delivery[318].

It has generally been accepted that it is the responsibility of the state, through the health authority, to ensure that all children are seen and are offered appropriate health surveillance. This assumption is not shared by all countries. We could not resolve the question as to how much responsibility should be taken by parents as opposed to the state to ensure that their children receive appropriate health surveillance. We agreed on the importance of easy access to health care for all children.

Perceptions of child health services

Non-attendance at child health clinics, contrary to popular belief, is not confined to low social classes, though the reasons may be different among different social groups[319-21]. The time and place at which clinics are held, the length of waiting time, the value of information and advice offered, and the warmth or otherwise of the social environment in the clinic all influence use of the services[322,323]. There has been relatively little research into what services are *wanted* by the consumer and which of these would be *useful*. To a considerable extent, demand for these services is created by professionals[325]. More information is required on parents' perceptions of the individual services, treatment, and advice offered in child health clinics.

Diagnostic services

It is beyond the scope of this report to discuss in detail the organization of secondary care or consultant services. It is however essential that each district and health board should have a locally based handicap team and/or child development centre and there should be ready access to the various specialist services which may be required for children with complex handicaps. The referral criteria and the most appropriate route of referral for each suspected abnormality should be defined and the information should be available to each primary care team.

Aspects of organization

Some centralized collection of information is necessary so that those in charge of the community child health surveillance service can receive information by which they can judge the success of the programme. Delegation of responsibility is necessary in order to obtain the most efficient delivery of services to children in a particular neighbourhood. In each locality primary health care teams must assume responsibility for ensuring that all children are seen at the appropriate ages[325-8]. However, we suggest that one individual should take responsibility in each district or health board for oversight of the programme of surveillance. This proposal should be instituted as soon as possible in the case of screening for hearing loss and might well be investigated for other selected aspects of the programme.

It is important to define the terms monitoring, audit, and evaluation. These tend to be used interchangeably but in fact refer to different activities. The three terms are defined below.

Monitoring

Having defined the desired programme of child health surveillance, it is necessary to monitor progress, to determine whether the programme is being delivered to all children. Measures of delivery do not in themselves give information as to the value of the programme. It is also necessary to measure the quality of individual clinical performance. For example, there is no value in achieving 100 per cent coverage with regard to the eight-month screening test of hearing if the test itself is carried out incorrectly.

It is also important to monitor the amount of work generated by a surveillance programme, for example in terms of referrals to consultant clinics or of length of time on the waiting list for surgery.

Audit

Audit is a process which makes use of information gathered in order to examine critically the performance and achievements of the surveillance programme. Data collected by monitoring the service are of little value unless considered in the context of local policies and conditions.

It is difficult to measure the quality of clinical work. The following measures are suggested:

1. The age at which serious defects are diagnosed may be useful as an indicator of the alertness and competence of health staff although it is not always easy to specify this age precisely in the individual case.

2. The age at which intervention services are first offered may also be an indirect indicator of the quality of care, although excessively early intervention is not necessarily desirable in every case.

3. An efficient network, in which colleagues in health and education work well together, should be able to detect most of the children likely to need special education before the age of five. It may be useful to record the number of those children, needing special educational provision within the first two years at school, who had not previously been thought to have any major developmental problems. Such a measure would depend to some extent on local policies and it would be misleading to use it for comparisons between districts or health boards.

4. There is no easy measure of parental satisfaction regarding the care of a handicapped child, but feedback from parents is very useful in determining whether the aims of early detection and counselling are being met.

When information gathered by the monitoring process is used as a measure of performance, it must be in the context of an overall audit rather than as a single numerical measure of efficiency.

Evaluation

Neither monitoring nor audit provide information as to the value of the surveillance programme. It may work very efficiently within its defined aims yet be of no value because the wrong condition is being detected, or because the intervention offered is not effective. Evaluation involves basic research on such issues. Many of the questions that we have raised and that require evaluation are complex and could only be studied by properly planned and well-funded programmes. It is important to separate the monitoring and audit of the programme we have recommended, which we regard as a service function, from research aspects, which must be considered separately.

Research

The Faculty of Community Medicine has set up a separate working party to consider how the programme recommended in the present report may be implemented and monitored. In due course, this group will be in a position to define research priorities.

16

Knowledge and skills required for surveillance

We have described an approach to child health surveillance that does not depend upon the routine developmental examination of all children. It must not be assumed that this reduces the level of skill required. On the contrary, primary health care professionals must have a thorough knowledge of child development, both normal and abnormal, to form a basis for the exercise of clinical judgement[329,330].

We realize that each primary health care team will make its own decisions about the allocation of duties within the overall pattern of child health surveillance as defined by local policy. We do not think it is appropriate for us to specify which professionals should undertake individual tasks or the way in which the specified knowledge and competencies are acquired.

In the following paragraphs we will outline the skills and knowledge that must be acquired by all staff involved in the health care of children. These are considered under two headings:

1. Basic knowledge of child development and related topics, needed by all staff.
2. The skills required for performance of specific tasks. These skills may in many situations be shared between members of a health care team and will not necessarily all be required by every individual.

Knowledge of child health and development

All staff need to appreciate and absorb the philosophy of health promotion, and concepts of surveillance, screening, and health education. They must have a basic knowledge of the following areas:

1. Child development, including normal variation, influences on development, stability, and change in development.
2. Atypical patterns of motor development and language acquisition.
3. The emergence of visual and auditory abilities.
4. The role and value of various forms of intervention.
5. Parental behaviour and responses when confronted with developmental problems in their children.
6. Relationships between local child health services and other agencies.
7. Roles and skills of professional colleagues.
8. Content and delivery of health education programmes.

The ability to evaluate a child's development is improved by experience. It is necessary to see a number of children at various ages in order to establish one's personal framework of what is normal. When there is doubt as to whether a child's developmental progress is within normal limits, a further opinion should be considered. It is essential that staff receive adequate feedback from the specialists to whom they refer, so that their knowledge and confidence increase with each referral.

The skills required

The most important abilities to be acquired are:

(1) to ascertain the views of the parents about their child;
(2) to elicit an accurate developmental history;
(3) to observe the child's play and behaviour;
(4) to initiate appropriate discussion and interpretation; and
(5) to interpret the findings.

We do not wish to specify which or whether any developmental charts, tests, or scales should be used to aid observation and recording, though they undoubtedly are a necessary teaching aid. We do not think there is a need for a detailed developmental progress chart to be maintained for every child (see p. 78).

Staff should be able to:

1. Recognize deviant motor development as seen for example in cerebral palsy.
2. Respond appropriately in cases of severely delayed motor development.
3. Evaluate a child's progress in language acquisition and be familiar with the various features which may suggest the presence of a serious impairment requiring further assessment.
4. Decide whether a parent wants or needs help with a behavioural or emotional problem.

The detection of hearing loss requires the following skills:

1. Selection of high-risk infants who require detailed testing.
2. Explanation to parents of how to use a check list.
3. Correct performance of the distraction test of hearing.
4. Evaluation of the likelihood of hearing loss by means of relevant questions to parents.
5. Recognition of the behavioural and developmental problems that may suggest a hearing loss.
6. Correct use of a speech discrimination test such as the McCormick Toy Test and of a performance test.
7. Use of a sound level meter.
8. Performance and interpretation of a modified pure tone audiogram (the 'sweep' test).
9. In each of the above, deciding on appropriate further action.

The detection of visual defects requires the following skills:

1. Identification of high-risk infants who may need expert examination.

2. Evaluation of visual development by means of relevant questions to parents.
3. Recognition of the red reflex by ophthalmoscopy in the neonate.
4. Observation and interpretation of visual behaviour.
5. Detailed inspection of the eyes for anomalies.
6. Measurement of visual acuity using letter-matching and letter-naming tests.
7. Detection of deficiencies of colour discrimination using the Ishihara Test, followed by appropriate advice when abnormalities are found.
8. For those staff who wish to carry out examinations for other disorders, proficiency in the use of the examination techniques applied by orthoptists.

Growth monitoring requires: (1) an understanding of normal growth and its variations; (2) the ability to make accurate measurements of height, weight, and head circumference; (3) the ability to plot the result correctly on an appropriate chart and to decide on further action.

The recognition of congenital dislocation of the hip requires the ability to perform the Ortolani–Barlow manoeuvre, to distinguish 'clicks' from 'clunks', and when in doubt to refer appropriately. The ability to recognize the classical physical signs and the typical gait associated with dislocation of the hip is also needed.

We further emphasize the importance of access to a specialist clinic for regular supervision of children with neurological disease who are at high risk of dislocation of the hip.

Skill in complete physical examination is necessary for both the birth and six-week examinations. Thereafter, although complete examination is sometimes required, particular attention should be paid to auscultation of the heart (the ability to distinguish between innocent and pathological murmurs and to make appropriate referral decisions), and to correct examination for mal-descent of the testes.

The need for continuing education

All staff should have the opportunity to see children with each of the serious conditions affecting development. This may be achieved either by clinical demonstration or videotape recordings. Dislocation of the hip can be understood more effectively by the use of a model[49].

Finally, we wish to emphasize again the importance of continuing education in child health surveillance and child development, as in any other branch of professional practice. It is vital not only to make available a thorough initial training, but also to make it possible for staff to meet to exchange ideas and discuss problems, and to update their knowledge. This must not be regarded as an expensive luxury, but as an essential part of the service.

17

Summary of recommended screening procedures

We recommend the following core programme of surveillance for all children. It incorporates those screening procedures which we believe can be supported in the light of the available evidence. In individual cases, parental concern or professional judgement may dictate that the child is seen on more or different occasions. We emphasize again that detection of defects is only one of the goals of surveillance (Chapters 4 and 13). A high uptake of immunization and an active programme of health education, accident prevention etc. are an intrinsic part of this programme.

Those procedures that fulfil the criteria for screening tests are *italicized*. It is assumed that more detailed evaluation will be offered for any child who has a positive screening test or whose health or development is causing concern to either parent or professional.

Neonatal examination. Review of family history, pregnancy, and birth. Any concerns expressed by parents. *Full physical examination, including weight and head circumference. Check for congenital dislocation of hips (CDH) and testicular descent. Inspect eyes, view red reflex of fundus with ophthalmoscope,* but do not attempt fundoscopy. If *high risk category* for hearing defect, consider *ARC or BSER* test of hearing. *PKU and thyroid* tests to be done at usual time.

At discharge or within ten days. Check *hips* again.

Six weeks. Check history and ask about parental concerns. *Physical examination, weight, and head circumference. Check for CDH.* Enquire particularly about concerns regarding vision and hearing. *Inspect eyes.* Do not attempt hearing test but check again whether baby is in *high-risk category for hearing loss* and refer if necessary. Give parents check-list of advice for detection of hearing loss ('Hints for Parents') (p. 65).

Eight months (range 7–9 months). Enquire about parental concerns regarding health and development. Ask specifically about vision and hearing. Check weight if parents request or if indicated. Look for evidence of *CDH.* Check for *testicular descent.* Observe visual behaviour and look for squint. Carry out *distraction test of hearing.*

Twenty-one months (range 18–24 months). Enquire about parental concerns, particularly regarding behaviour, vision, and hearing. Confirm that child is *walking with normal gait* (p. 21), is beginning to say words, and is understanding when spoken to. Do not attempt formal tests of vision or hearing. Arrange detailed assessment if either are in doubt. Remember high prevalence of iron deficiency anaemia at this age (p. 35).

Thirty-nine months (range 36–42 months). Ask about vision, squint, hearing, behaviour, and development. If any concerns, discuss with the parent whether the child is likely to have any special educational problems or needs and arrange further action as appropriate. Measure *height* and plot on chart. Check for *testicular descent* (if not checked on any other occasion since eight months). If indicated, perform or arrange hearing test.

Five years (school entry—range approximately 48–66 months). Enquire about parental and teacher concerns. Review pre-school records. *Physical examination,* including *auscultation of heart,* if specific indication, or if no record available to confirm previous medical care. Measure *height* and plot on chart. Check *vision* using Snellen chart. Check hearing by '*sweep*' test.

School years. Further *visual acuity check at ages eight, eleven, and fourteen.* Test *colour vision* using Ishihara plates at age 11. Repeat height measurement if indicated (p. 43).

References

1. Senturia, Y. D. and Peckham, C. S. (1987). Pre-schcol immunization; the importance of achieving adequate uptake. *Children and Society* 1, 198–209.
2. Jarman, B., Bosanquet, N., Rice, P., Dollimore, N., and Leese, B. (1988). Uptake of immunization in district health authorities in England. *British Medical Journal* 296, 1775–8.
3. Wells, N. (1987). Immunization—where do we go from here? In *Progress in child health* (ed. J. A. Macfarlane), Vol. 3. Churchill Livingstone, Edinburgh.
4. Colver, A. F. and Steiner, H. (1986). Health surveillance of preschool children. *British Medical Journal* 293, 258–60.
5. World Health Organization (1981). Early detection of handicap in children. Report of a Working Group. WHO, Geneva.
6. US Congress, Office of Technology Assessment (1988). Healthy children: investing in the future. OTA-H-345. US Government Printing Office, Washington DC.
7. Committee on Children with Disabilities (1986). Screening for developmental disabilities. *Pediatrics* 78, 526–8.
8. Kohler, L. (1984). Early detection and screening programmes for children in Sweden. In *Progress in child health* (ed. J. A. Macfarlane), Vol. 1. Churchill Livingstone, Edinburgh.
9. de Winter, M. (1985). Early detection of abnormality in Dutch children and its drawbacks. In *Progress in child health* (ed. J. A. Macfarlane), Vol. 2. Churchill Livingstone, Edinburgh.
10. Jaffe, M., Harel, J., Goldberg, A., Rudolph-Schnitzer, M., and Winter, S. T. (1980). The use of the Denver developmental screening test in infant welfare clinics. *Developmental Medicine and Child Neurology* 22, 55–60.
11. Macfarlane, J. A. and Pillay, U. (1984). Who does what, and how much in the preschool child health services in England. *British Medical Journal* 289, 851–2.
12. Stewart-Brown, S. and Haslum, M. N. (1987). Screening for hearing loss in childhood: a study of national practice. *British Medical Journal* 294, 1386–8.

13. Holt, K. (1974). Screening for disease in infancy and childhood. *Lancet* ii, 2057–9.
14. Dworkin, P. H. British and American recommendations for developmental monitoring—are they compatible? (In preparation.)
15. Curtis-Jenkins, G. H. *et al.* (1978). Developmental surveillance in general practice. *British Medical Journal* i, 1537–40.
16. Gilbert, J. R. *et al.* (1984). How many well-baby visits are necessary in the first 2 years of life? *Canadian Medical Association Journal* **130**, 857–61.
17. Hoekelman, R. A. (1975). What constitutes adequate well-baby care? *Pediatrics* **55**, 313–25.
18. Yankauer, A. (1973). Child health supervision—is it worth it? *Pediatrics* **52**, 272–9.
19. Hutchinson, T. and Nicoll, A. (1988). Developmental screening and surveillance. *British Journal of Hospital Medicine* **39**, 22–9.
20. Hendrickse, W. A. (1982). How effective are our child health clinics? *British Medical Journal* **284**, 575–7 (see also same volume, pp. 819–21).
21. Baird, G. and Hall, D. M. B. (1985). Developmental paediatrics in primary care; what should we teach? *British Medical Journal* **291**, 583–6.
22. Stacey, M. and Graham, H. (1984). Socio-economic factors related to child health. In *Progress in child health* (ed. J. A. Macfarlane), Vol. 1. Churchill Livingstone, Edinburgh.
23. Department of Education and Science (1978). Warnock Report on Special Educational Needs. HMSO, London.
24. Locke, A. (1978). The case against assessment. *Bulletin of the British Psychological Society* **31**, 322–4.
25. Murphy, G. (1987). Are intelligence tests outmoded? *Archives of Disease in Childhood* **62**, 773–5.
26. Berger, M. and Yule, W. (1985). IQ tests and assessment. In *Mental deficiency: the changing outlook* (ed. A. M. Clarke, A. D. B. Clarke, and J. M. Berg), 4th edn, pp. 53–96. Methuen, London and Free Press, New York.
27. World Health Organization (1986). Charter for health promotion. WHO, Regional Office for Europe.
28. World Health Organization (1981). *International classification of impairments, disabilities and handicaps. A manual of classification relating to the consequence of disease.* WHO, Geneva.
29. Shearer, A. (1981). *Disability—whose handicap?* Blackwell, Oxford.
30. Wilson, J. M. G. and Jungner, G. (1968). Principles and practice of screening for disease. Public Health Papers No. 34. WHO, Geneva.

31. Cochrane, A. and Holland, W. (1969). Validation of screening procedures. *British Medical Bulletin* 27, 3–8.
32. Rose, G. (1978). Epidemiology for the uninitiated: screening. *British Medical Journal* 2, 1417–18.
33. Palfrey, J. S., Singer, J. D., Walker, D. K., and Butler, J. A. (1987). Early identification of childrens' special needs; a study in five metropolitan communities. *Journal of Pediatrics* 111, 651–9.
34. Robson, P. (1987). Lower limb deformity and prevention of scoliosis in cerebral palsy. *Archives of Disease in Childhood* 62, 547–8.
35. Guralnick, M. J. and Bennett, F. C. (1987). *The effectiveness of early intervention for at-risk and handicapped children.* Academic Press, New York.
36. Dowling, S. (1985). The voluntary sector and child health. In *Progress in child health* (ed. J. A. Macfarlane), Vol. 2. Churchill Livingstone, Edinburgh.
37. Cunningham, C. C., Morgan, P. A., and McGucken, R. B. (1984). Down's syndrome: is dissatisfaction with disclosure of diagnosis inevitable? *Developmental Medicine and Child Neurology* 26, 33–9.
38. Quine, L. and Pahl, J. (1987). First diagnosis of severe handicap; a study of parental reactions. *Developmental Medicine and Child Neurology* 29, 232–42.
39. McConachie, H., Lingham, S., Stiff, B., and Holt, K. S. (1988). Giving assessment reports to parents. *Archives of Disease in Childhood* 63, 209–10.
40. Anderson, F. P. (1970). Evaluation of the routine physical examination of infants in the first year of life. *Pediatrics* 45, 950–64.
41. Hall, D. M. B. and Hall, S. M. (1988). Early detection of vision defects in infancy. *British Medical Journal* 296, 823–4.
42. Department of Health and Social Security (1972). *Report of a working group on risk registers.* HMSO, London.
43. Williams, P. R. (1985). Opportunistic surveillance of children. *Journal of the Royal College of General Practitioners* 35, 248–50.
44. Houston, H. L. A. and Davis, R. H. (1985). Opportunistic surveillance of child development in primary care: is it feasible? *Journal of the Royal College of General Practitioners* 35, 77–9.
45. Drillien, C. and Drummond, M. (1983). Developmental screening and the child with special needs. *Clinics in Developmental Medicine*, Vol. 86. Heinemann, London.
46. Goffman, E. (1963). Stigma—notes on the management of spoiled identity. Penguin, Harmondsworth.
47. Cox, A. D. (1988). Maternal depression and impact on childrens' development. *Archives of Disease in Childhood* 63, 90–5.

48. Spencer, N. J. (1984). Parents' recognition of the ill child. In *Progress in child health* (ed. J. A. Macfarlane), Vol. 1. Churchill Livingstone, Edinburgh.
49. Department of Health and Social Security (1986). *Screening for the detection of congenital dislocation of the hip.* HMSO, London.
50. Dunn, P. M. Screening for congenital dislocation of the hip. In *Progress in child health* (ed. J. A. Macfarlane), Vol. 3. Churchill Livingstone, Edinburgh.
51. Fixsen, J. (1985). Congenital dislocation of the hip. In *Progress in child health* (ed. J. A. Macfarlane), Vol. 2. Churchill Livingstone, Edinburgh.
52. Dwyer, N. St. J. P. (1987). Congenital dislocation of the hip; to screen or not to screen? *Archives of Disease in Childhood* 62, 635–7.
53. Knox, E. G., Armstrong, E. H., and Lancashire, R. J. (1987). Effectiveness of screening for congenital dislocation of the hip. *Journal of Epidemiology and Community Health* 41, 283–9.
54. Heikkila, E., Ryooppy, S., and Louhimo, I. (1984). Late diagnosis in congenital dislocation of the hip. *Acta Orthopaedica Scandinavica* 55, 256–60.
55. Frankenburg, W. K. (1981). To screen or not to screen. Congenital dislocation of the hip. *American Journal of Public Health* 71, 1311–12.
56. Berman, L. and Klenerman, L. (1986). Ultrasound screening for hip abnormalities; preliminary findings in 1001 neonates. *British Medical Journal* 293, 719–22.
57. Scott, D. J., Rigby, M. L., Miller, G. A. H., and Shinebourne, E. A. (1984). The presentation of symptomatic heart disease in infancy based on 10 years' experience (1973–82). Implications for the provision of services. *British Heart Journal* 52, 248–57.
58. Rosenthal, A. (1984). How to distinguish between innocent and pathologic murmurs in childhood. *Pediatric Clinics of North America* 31, 1229–40.
59. Newburger, J. W., Rosenthal, A., Williams, R. G., Fellows, K., and Miettinen, O. S. Invasive tests in the initial evaluation of heart murmurs in children. *New England Journal of Medicine* 308, 61–4.
60. Raftery, E. B. and Holland, W. W. (1966). Examination of the heart: an investigation into variation. *American Journal of Epidemiology* 85, 438–44.
61. McLaren, M. J., Lachman, A. S., Pocock, W. A., and Barlow, J. B. (1980). Innocent murmurs and third heart sounds in Black schoolchildren. *British Heart Journal* 43, 67–73.
62. Park, S. C. *et al.* (1977). Down's syndrome with congenital heart malformation. *American Journal of Diseases of Children* 131, 29–33.

63. de Swiet, M. (1986). The epidemiology of hypertension in children. *British Medical Bulletin* **42**, 172–5.

64. Gill, D. G., Mendes da Costa, B., Cameron, J. S., Joseph, M. C., Ogg, O. S., and Chantler, C. (1976). Analysis of 100 children with severe and persistent hypertension. *Archives of Disease in Childhood* **51**, 951–6.

65. Pollock, E., Wines, W., and Hall, D. (1981). A survey of blood pressure in 10-year-old children of a health district together with a consideration of screening policy for hypertension. *Community Medicine* **3**, 199–204.

66. Fixler, D. E. and Pennock, W. (1983). Validity of mass blood pressure screening in children. *Pediatrics* **72**, 459–63.

67. Dillon, M. J. (1988). Blood pressure. *Archives of Disease in Childhood* **63**, 347–9.

68. Godfrey, S. (1985). What is asthma? *Archives of Disease in Childhood* **60**, 997–1000.

69. Martin, A. J., McClelland, L. A., Landau, L. I., and Phelan, P. D. (1980). The natural history of asthma to adult life. *British Medical Journal* **280**, 1397–400.

70. Mitchell, E. A., Ferguson, V., and Norwood, M. (1986). Asthma education by community child health nurses. *Archives of Disease in Childhood* **61**, 1184–9.

71. Speight, A. N. P., Lee, D. A., and Hey, E. N. (1983). Under-diagnosis and undertreatment of asthma in childhood. *British Medical Journal* **286**, 1253–6.

72. Anderson, H. R., Bailey, P. A., Cooper, J. S., Palmer, J. C., and West, S. (1983). Morbidity and school absence caused by asthma and wheezing illness. *Archives of Disease in Childhood* **58**, 777–84.

73. Anderson, H. R., Bailey, P. A., Cooper, J. S., Palmer, J. C., and West, S. (1983). Medical care of asthma and wheezing illness in children: a community survey. *Journal of Epidemiology and Community Health* **37**, 180–6.

74. Beer, S., Laver, J., Karpuch, J., Chabut, S., Aladjem, M. (1987). Prodromal features of asthma. *Archives of Disease in Childhood* **62**, 345–8.

75. Tanakas, J. S., Milner, R. D. G., Bannister, O. M., and Boon, A. W. (1988). Free-running asthma screening test. *Archives of Disease in Childhood* **63**, 261–5.

76. John Radcliffe Hospital Cryptorchidism Study Group (1986). Cryptorchidism: an apparent substantial increase since 1960. *British Medical Journal* **293**, 1404–6.

77. Chilvers, C., Dudley, N. E., Gough, M. H., Jackson, M. B., and Pike, M. C. (1986). Undescended testis: the effect of treatment on

subsequent risk of subfertility and malignancy. *Journal of Pediatric Surgery* **21**, 691–6.

78. Scorer, C. G. and Farrington, G. H. (1971). *Congenital deformities of the testis and epididymis.* Butterworth, London.
79. Depue, R. H. (1984). Maternal and gestational factors affecting the risk of cryptorchidism and inguinal hernia. *International Journal of Epidemiology* **13**, 311–18.
80. Atwell, J. D. (1985). Ascent of the testis: fact or fiction? *British Journal of Urology* **57**, 474–7.
81. John Radcliffe Hospital Cryptorchidism Study Group (1986). Boys with late descending testes: the source of cases of 'retractile testes' undergoing orchidopexy? *British Medical Journal* **293**, 789–90.
82. John Radcliffe Hospital Cryptorchidism Study Group (1988). Clinical diagnosis of cryptorchidism. *Archives of Disease in Childhood* **63**, 587–91.
83. The British Orthopaedic Association and the British Scoliosis Society (1983). School screening for scoliosis. *British Medical Journal* **287**, 963–4.
84. Goldberg, C., Fogart, E. E., Blake, N. S., Dowling, F., and Regan, B. F. (1983). School scoliosis screening: a review of 21 000 children. *Irish Medical Journal* **76**, 247–9.
85. Bunnell, W. P. (1982). A study of the natural history of idiopathic scoliosis. *Proceedings of the Scoliosis Research Society* (Denver), p. 54.
86. Turcotte, F. *et al.* (1981). Scoliosis screening revisited. *Proceedings of the Scoliosis Research Society* (Denver), pp. 83–4.
87. Weidenbaum, M. and Riseborough, E. (1981). The effect of school screening on the diagnosis and treatment of scoliosis. *Proceedings of the Scoliosis Research Society* (Denver), pp. 84–5.
88. Leaver, J. M., Alvik, A., and Warren, M. D. (1982). Prescriptive screening for adolescent idiopathic scoliosis. A review of the evidence. *International Journal of Epidemiology* **11**, 101–11.
89. Asher, M. A. (1986). Screening for congenital dislocation of the hip, scoliosis and other abnormalities affecting the musculoskeletal system. *Pediatric Clinics of North America* **33**, 1335–53.
90. Lindsay, G., ed. (1984). *Screening for children with special needs.* Croom Helm, London.
91. Grant, D. B. and Smith, I. (1988). Survey of neonatal screening for primary hypothyroidism in England, Wales and Northern Ireland 1982–4. *British Medical Journal* **296**, 1355–8.
92. Barnes, N. D. (1985). Screening for congenital hypothyroidism; the first decade. *Archives of Disease in Childhood* **60**, 587–92.

93. Rosenthal, M., Addison, G. M., and Price, D. A. (1988). Congenital hypothyroidism; increased incidence in Asian families. *Archives of Disease in Childhood* **63**, 790–3.

94. Fort, P., Lifshitz, F., and Bellisario, R. (1984). Abnormalities of thyroid function in infants with Down's syndrome. *Journal of Pediatrics* **104**, 545–50.

95. Dodge, J. A. and Ryley, H. C. (1982). Screening for cystic fibrosis. *Archives of Disease in Childhood* **57**, 774–80.

96. Brock, D. H. J. (1988). Prenatal diagnosis of cystic fibrosis. *Archives of Disease in Childhood* **63**, 701–4.

97. Gardner-Medwin, D. (1979). Controversies about muscular dystrophy (1) Neonatal screening. *Developmental Medicine and Child Neurology* **21**, 390–3.

98. Crisp, D. E., Ziter, F. A., and Bray, P. F. (1982). Diagnostic delay in Duchenne's muscular dystrophy. *Journal of the American Medical Association* **247**, 478–80.

99. Chaplais, J. de Z. (1984). The late walking child. In *Progress in Child Health* (ed. J. A. Macfarlane), Vol. 1. Churchill Livingstone, Edinburgh.

100. White, R. H. R. (1987). Management of urinary tract infection. *Archives of Disease in Childhood* **62**, 421–7.

101. World Health Organization Working Group (1982). Hereditary anaemias; genetic basis, clinical features, diagnosis and treatment. *WHO Bulletin* **60**, 643–60.

102. World Health Organization (1983). Memorandum from a WHO meeting: community control of hereditary anaemias. *WHO Bulletin* **61**, 63–80.

103. Wethers, D. L. and Grover, R. (1986). Screening the newborn for sickle cell disease: is it worth the effort? In *Genetic disease; screening and management* (ed. T. P. Carter and A. M. Willey). Alan R. Liss, New York.

104. Gaston, M. H. *et al.* (1986). Prophylaxis with oral penicillin in children with sickle cell anemia. *New England Journal of Medicine* **314**, 1593–9.

105. Anon. (leading article) (1986). Penicillin prophylaxis for babies with sickle-cell disease. *Lancet* 20–27 Dec., 1432–3.

106. Griffiths, P. D., Mann, J. R., Darbyshire, P. J., and Green, A. (1988). Evaluation of eight and a half years of neonatal screening for haemoglobinopathies in Birmingham. *British Medical Journal* **296**, 1583–5.

107. Modell, B., Petrou, M., Ward, R. H. T., Fairweather, D. V. I., Rodeck, C., Varnavides, L. A., and White, J. M. (1984). Effect of

fetal diagnostic testing on birth-rate of thalassaemia major in Britain. *Lancet* 15 Dec., 1383–6.

108. Franklin, I. M. (1988). Services for sickle cell disease; unified approach needed. *British Medical Journal* **296**, 592.

109. Prashar, U., Anionwu, E., Brozovic, M. (1985). *Sickle cell anaemia—who cares? A survey in screening and counselling facilities in England.* Runnymede Trust, London.

110. Anon. (leading article) (1987). Iron deficiency. Time for a community campaign? *Lancet* 17 Jan., 141–2.

111. Lozoff, B., *et al.* (1982). Iron deficiency anemia and iron therapy: effects on infant developmental test performance. *Pediatrics* **79**, 981–95.

112. Soemantri, A. G., Pollitt, E., and Kim, I. (1985). Iron deficiency anemia and educational achievement. *American Journal of Clinical Nutrition* **42**, 1221–8.

113. Ankett, M. A., Parks, Y. A., Scott, P. H., and Wharton, B. A. (1986). Treatment with iron increases weight gain and psychomotor development. *Archives of Disease in Childhood* **61**, 849–57.

114. Deinard, A. S. *et al.* (1986). Cognitive deficits in iron—deficient and iron-deficient anemic children. *Pediatrics* **108**, 681–9.

115. James, J., Evans, J., Male, P., Pallister, C., Hendrikz, J. K., and Oakhill, A. (1988). Iron deficiency in inner city pre-school children: development of a general practice screening programme. *Journal of the Royal College of General Practitioners* **38**, 250–2.

116. Reeves, J. D. *et al.* (1983). Iron deficiency in health and disease. *Advances in Pediatrics* **30**, 281–320.

117. Lloyd, J. K. and West, R. J. (1986). Childhood prevention of coronary heart disease. *Postgraduate Medical Journal* **62**, 97–100.

118. Lipid Research Clinics Program (1984). The lipid research clinics' coronary primary prevention trials results. (i) Reduction in incidence of coronary heart disease. (ii) The relationship of reduction in incidence of coronary heart disease to cholesterol lowering. *Journal of the American Medical Association* **251**, 351–74.

119. Frank, G. C., Berenson, G. S., and Webber, L. S. (1978). Dietary studies and its relationship of diet to cardiovascular disease risk factor variables in 10-year-old children. The Bogalusa heart study. *American Journal of Clinical Nutrition* **31**, 328–40.

120. Stamler, J. and Stamler, R. (1984). Intervention for the prevention and control of hypertension in atherosclerotic disease. USA and international experience. *American Journal of Medicine* **76**, 13–36.

121. Collacott, R. A. (leading article) (1987). Atlanto-axial instability in Down's syndrome. *British Medical Journal* **294**, 988–9.

122. Evans, T. J. and Davies, D. P. (1977). Failure to thrive at the breast. *Archives of Disease in Childhood* **52**, 974–5.

123. Goldson, E. (1987). Failure to thrive; an old problem re-visited. In *Progress in child health* (ed. J. A. Macfarlane), Vol. 3. Churchill Livingstone, Edinburgh.

124. Dowdney, L., Skuse, D., Heptinstall, E., Puckering, C., and Zur-Szpiro, S. (1987). Growth retardation and developmental delay amongst inner-city children. *Journal of Child Psychology and Psychiatry* **28**, 529–41.

125. Heptinstall, E., Puckering, C., Skuse, D., Dowdney, L., and Zur-Szpiro, S. (1987). Nutrition and meal-time behaviour in families of growth-retarded children. *Human Nutrition: Applied Nutrition* **41**, 390–402.

126. Mitchell, W. G., Gorrell, R. W., and Greenberg, R. A. (1980). Failure to thrive; a study in a primary care setting; epidemiology and follow-up. *Pediatrics* **65**, 971–7.

127. Emery, J. L., Waite, A. J., Carpenter, R. G., Limerick, S. R., and Blake, D. (1985). Apnoea monitors compared with weighing scales for siblings after cot death. *Archives of Disease in Childhood* **60**, 1055–60.

128. Carpenter, R. G. *et al.* (1986). Prevention of unexpected infant death; evaluation of the first seven years of the Sheffield programme. *Lancet* 2 April, 723–7.

129. Waite, A. J. (1987). The care of siblings of sudden infant death syndrome babies. In *Progress in Child Health* (ed. J. A. Macfarlane), Vol. 3. Churchill Livingstone, Edinburgh.

130. Woolston, J. W. (1987). Obesity in infancy and early childhood. *Journal of the American Academy of Child and Adolescent Psychiatry* **26**, 123–6.

131. Poskitt, E. M. E. (1987). Management of obesity. *Archives of Disease in Childhood* **62**, 305–10.

132. Brook, C. D. G. (1982). *Growth assessment in childhood and adolescence*. Blackwell, Oxford.

133. Law, C. M. (1987). The disability of short stature. *Archives of Disease in Childhood* **62**, 855–9.

134. Aynsley Green, A. and Macfarlane, J. A. (1983). Method for the earlier recognition of abnormal stature. *Archives of Disease in Childhood* **58**, 535–7.

135. Buchanan, C. R., Law, C. M., and Milner, R. D. G. (1987). Growth hormone in short, slowly growing children and those with Turner's syndrome. *Archives of Disease in Childhood* **62**, 912–16.

136. Lyon, A. J., Preece, M. A., and Grant, D. B. (1985). Growth curve for girls with Turner syndrome. *Archives of Disease in Childhood* **60**, 932–5.

137. Day, R. E. and Schutt, W. H. (1979). Normal children with large heads; benign familial megalencephaly. *Archives of Disease in Childhood* **54**, 512–17.

138. Lorber, J. and Priestley, B. L. (1981). Children with large heads. *Developmental Medicine and Child Neurology* **23**, 494–504.

139. Dennis, M., Fitz, C. R., Oxtley, C. T., Sugar, J., Harwood-Nash, D. C., Hendrick, E. B., Hoffman, J. J., and Humphreys, R. P. (1981). The intelligence of hydrocephalic children. *Archives of Neurology* **38**, 607–15.

140. Robb, R. M. (1981). *Ophthalmology for the pediatric practitioner.* Little Brown, Boston, Mass.

141. Smith, V. and Keen, J. (1979). *Visual handicap in children.* Clinics in developmental medicine No. 73. Spastics/Heinemann, London.

142. Taylor, D. and Rice, N. S. C. (1982). Congenital cataracts, a cause of preventable child blindness. *Archives of Disease in Childhood* **57**, 165–6.

143. Sonksen, P. M. (1982). The assessment of vision for development in severely visually handicapped babies. *Acta Ophthalmologica (Copenhagen)* Suppl. 157, 82–90.

144. Cashell, G. T. W. and Durran, I. N. (1980). *Handbook of orthoptic principles* (4th edn). Churchill Livingstone, Edinburgh.

145. Stewart-Brown, S. (1987). Visual defects in school children: screening policy and education implications. In *Progress in Child Health* (ed. J. A. Macfarlane), Vol. 3. Churchill Livingstone, Edinburgh.

146. Shaw, D. E., Minshull, C., Fielder, A. R., and Rosenthal, A. R. (1988). Amblyopia—factors affecting age of presentation. *Lancet*, 23 July, 207–9.

147. Eggers, H. M. and Blakemore, C. (1978). Physiologic basis of anisometropic amblyopia. *Science* **201**, 264–6.

148. Tommila, V. and Tarkkanen, A. (1981). Incidence of loss of vision in the healthy eye in amblyopia. *British Journal of Ophthalmology* **65**, 575–7.

149. Ingram, R. M., Holland, W. W., Walker, C., Wilson, J. M., Arnold, P. E., and Dally, S. (1986). Screening for visual defects in preschool children. *British Journal of Ophthalmology* **70**, 16–21.

150. Kohler, L. (1984). Early detection and screening programmes for children in Sweden. In *Progress in Child Health* (ed. J. A. Macfarlane), Vol. 1. Churchill Livingstone, Edinburgh.

151. Hall, S. M., Pugh, A. G., and Hall, D. M. B. (1982). Vision screening in the under-5s. *British Medical Journal* **285**, 1096-8.
152. Taylor, D. (1987). Screening for squint and poor vision. *Archives of Disease in Childhood* **62**, 982-3.
153. Atkinson, J., Braddick, O., Pimm-Smith, E., Ayling, L., and Sawyer, R. (1981). Does the Catford drum give an accurate assessment of acuity? *British Journal of Ophthalmology* **65**, 652-6.
154. Atkinson, J., Braddick, O. J., Durden, K., Watson, P. G., and Atkinson, S. (1984). Screening for refractive errors in 6-9-month-old infants by photorefraction. *British Journal of Ophthalmology* **68**, 105-12.
155. Atkinson, J., Braddick, O. J., and Wattam-Bell, J. (1987). Photo-refractive screening of infants and effects of refractive correction. *Investigative Ophthalmology and Vision Science* **28**, 399.
156. Kaakinen, K. (1978). Screening by simultaneous photography of corneal and fundus reflexes. *Acta Ophthalmologica* **57**, 161.
157. Friendly, D. S. (1987). Amblyopia: definition, classification, diagnosis, and management. *Pediatric Clinics of North America* **34**, 1389-401; 1425-37.
158. Hammond, R. S. and Schmidt, P. P. (1986). A random dot E stereogram for the vision screening of children. *Archives of Ophthalmology* **104**, 54-60.
159. Sonksen, P. M. and Macrae, A. J. (1987). Vision for coloured pictures at different acuities; the Sonksen picture guide to visual function. *Developmental Medicine and Child Neurology* **29**, 337-47.
160. Hilton, A. P. and Stanley, J. C. (1972). Pitfalls in testing children's vision by the Sheridan-Gardner single optotype method. *British Journal of Ophthalmology* **56**, 135-9.
161. Egan, D. F. and Brown, R. (1984). Vision testing of young children in the age range 18 months to 4½ years. *Child Care, Health and Development* **10**, 381-90.
162. Stewart-Brown, S. L., Haslum, M. N., and Howlett, B. (1988). Preschool vision screening; a service in need of rationalisation. *Archives of Disease in Childhood* **63**, 356-9.
163. Catford, J. C., Absolon, M. J., and Mill, O. A. (1984). Squints— a sideways look. In *Progress in Child Health* (ed. J. A. Macfarlane), Vol. 1. Churchill Livingstone, Edinburgh.
164. Ingram, R. M. (1979). Refraction as a means of predicting squint or amblyopia in preschool siblings of children known to have these defects. *British Journal of Ophthalmology* **63**, 238-42.
165. Ingram, R. M., Walker, C., Wilson, J. M., Arnold, P. E., Lucas, J., and Dally, S. (1985). A first attempt to prevent squint and ambly-

opia by spectacle córrection of abnormal refractions from age one year. *British Journal of Ophthalmology* **69**, 851–3.

166. Bankes, J. L. K. (1974). Eye defects of mentally handicapped children. *British Medical Journal* **ii**, 533–5.

167. Feldman, W. *et al.* (1980). Effects of preschool screening for vision and hearing on prevalence of vision and hearing problems 6–12 months later. *Lancet* **i**, 1014–16.

168. Hill, A. R. (1984). Defective colour vision in children. In *Progress in Child Health* (ed. J. A. Macfarlane), Vol. 1. Churchill Livingstone, Edinburgh.

169. Mandola, J. (1965). The role of colour vision anomalies in elementary school achievement. *Journal of School Health* **39**, 633–6.

170. Bacon, L. (1971). Colour vision defect—an educational handicap. *Medical Officer* **125**, 199–209.

171. Konigsmark, B. W. and Gorlin, R. J. (1976). *Genetic and metabolic deafness.* W. B. Saunders, Philadelphia.

172. Symposium on Pediatric Otolaryngology (1987). *Pediatric Clinics of North America* **28**, 4.

173. Sade, J. (1979). *Secretory otitis media and its sequelae.* Monographs in Clinical Otolaryngology, No. 1. Churchill Livingstone, Edinburgh.

174. Martin, J. A. M. and Moore, W. J. (1979). *Childhood deafness in the European community.* Commission of the European Communities, HMSO (EUR 6413), London.

175. Yeates, S. (1981). *Development of hearing.* MTP Press, Lancaster.

176. Lane, H. (1984). *When the mind hears.* Random House, New York.

177. Brugge, J. F. (1983). Development of the lower brainstem auditory nuclei. In *Development of auditory and vestibular systems* (ed. R. Romand), pp. 111–20. Academic Press, New York.

178. Hall, D. M. B. and Hill, P. (1986). When does secretory otitis media affect language development? *Archives of Disease in Childhood* **61**, 42–7.

179. Paradise, J. L. (1981). Otitis media during early life; how hazardous to development? A critical review of the evidence. *Pediatrics* **68**, 869–73.

180. Grant, H. R., Quiney, R. E., Mercer, D. M., and Lodge, S. (1988). Cleft palate and glue ear. *Archives of Disease in Childhood* **63**, 176–9.

181. Black, N. A. (1985). Surgery for glue ear—the determinants of an epidemic. In *Progress in Child Health* (ed. J. A. Macfarlane), Vol. 2. Churchill Livingstone, Edinburgh.

182. Newton, V. E. (1985). Aetiology of bilateral sensori-neural hearing loss in young children. *Journal of Laryngology and Otology* Supplement 10.
183. Bhattacharya, J., Bennett, M. J., and Tucker, S. M. (1984). Long term follow-up for newborns tested with the auditory response cradle. *Archives of Disease in Childhood* **59**, 504–11.
184. Hyde, M. K., Riko, K., Corbin, H., Moroso, M., and Alberti, P. W. (1983). A neonatal hearing screening research program using brainstem electric response audiometry. *Journal of Otolaryngology* **13**, 49–54.
185. Kemp, D. T., Bray, P., Alexander, L., and Brown, A. M. (1986). Acoustic emission cochleography—practical aspects. *Scandinavian Audiology* Suppl. 25, 71–94.
186. Swigart, E. T. (1986). *Neonatal hearing screening.* Taylor and Francis, London.
187. Hall, D. M. B. and Garner, J. (1988). The feasibility of screening all neonates for hearing loss. *Archives of Disease in Childhood* **63**, 652–3.
188. Hitchings, V. and Haggard, M. P. (1983). Incorporation of parental suspicions in screening infants. *British Journal of Audiology* **17**, 71–5.
189. Department of Health and Social Security (1981). *The ACSHIP Report* (Chairman J. C. Balantyne). Advisory committee on services for hearing impaired people. Report of the sub-committee for hearing impaired children. DHSS.
190. McCormick, B. (1988). *Screening for hearing impairment in young children.* Croom Helm, London.
191. McCormick, B. (1977). The toy discrimination test: an aid for screening the hearing of children above a mental age of two years. *Public Health* **91**, 67–9.
192. Boothman, R. and Orr, N. (1978). Screening for deafness in the first year of life. *Archives of Disease in Childhood* **53**, 570–3.
193. McCormick, B. (1983). Hearing screening by health visitors; a critical appraisal of the distraction test. *Health Visitor* **56**, 449–51.
194. Nietupska, O. and Harding, N. (1982). Auditory screening of school children; fact or fallacy? *British Medical Journal* **284**, 717–20.
195. Fisch, L. (1981). Development of school screening audiometry. *British Journal of Audiology* **15**, 87–95.
196. Hallett, C. P. and Gibbs, A. C. C. (1983). The effect of ambient noise and other variables on pure tone threshold screening in a population of primary school entrants. *British Journal of Audiology* **17**, 183–90.

197. Jaffa, E. (1977). Learning disorders in young schoolchildren: is neurodevelopmental screening of value? *Public Health* **91**, 237–47.

198. Court, S. D. M. (1976). *Fit for the future. Report of the committee on child health services.* HMSO, London.

199. Newson, E. (1978). Unreasonable care: the establishment of self-hood. In *Human values. Lectures of the Royal Institute of Philosophy* (ed. G. Vesey). Harvester Press, England.

200. Hart, H., Bax, M., and Jenkins, S. (1978). The value of a developmental history. *Developmental Medicine and Child Neurology* **20**, 442.

201. Carey, W. B. (1982). Validity of parental assessment of development and behaviour. *American Journal of Diseases of Children* **136**, 97–9.

202. Egan, D. F. (1969). *Developmental screening 0–5 years.* Clinics in Developmental Medicine, No. 30. Spastics Society/Heinemann, London.

203. Bellman, M. H., Rawson, N. S., Wadsworth, J., Ross, E. M., Cameron, S., and Miller, D. L. (1985). A developmental test based on the STYCAR sequences used in the National Childhood Encephalopathy study. *Child Care, Health and Development* **11**, 309–23.

204. Sonnander, K. (1987). Parental developmental assessment of 18-month-old children; reliability and predictive value. *Developmental Medicine and Child Neurology* **29**, 351–62.

205. Camp, B. W. *et al.* (1977). Preschool developmental testing in prediction of school problems. *Clinical Pediatrics* **16**, 257–63.

206. Borowitz, K. C. and Glascoe, F. P. (1986). Sensitivity of the Denver developmental screening test in speech and language screening. *Pediatrics* **78**, 1075–8.

207. Sturner, R. A., Green, J. A., and Funk, S. G. (1985). Preschool Denver developmental screening test as a predictor of late school problems. *Pediatrics* **107**, 615–21.

208. Cadman, D., Chambers, L. W., Walter, S. D., Feldman, W., Smith, K., and Ferguson, R. (1984). Usefulness of DDST to predict kindergarten problems in a general community population. *American Journal of Public Health* **74**, 1093–7.

209. Knobloch, H., Stevens, F., and Malone, A. F. (1980). Manual of Development Diagnosis. Harper and Row, Hagerstown.

210. Eu, B. S. L. (1986). Evaluation of a developmental screening system for use by child health nurses. *Archives of Disease in Childhood* **61**, 34–41.

211. Rutter, M. (1987). Assessment of language disorders. In *Language*

development and disorders (ed. W. Yule and M. Rutter), pp. 295–311. Clinics in Developmental Medicine, Nos 101, 102. Mackeith Press/ Blackwell, Oxford.

212. Silva, P. A. (1981). Predictive validity of a simple two-item screening test for three-year olds. *New Zealand Medical Journal* **93**, 39–41.

213. Bax, M. (1981). The intimate relationship of health, development, and behaviour in the young child. In *Infants at risk: assessment and intervention* (ed. C. C. Brown). Pediatric Round Table No. 5. Johnson and Johnson, New Jersey.

214. Royal College of General Practitioners (1982). Working party on prevention: report from general practice 22. *Healthier children— thinking prevention.* Royal College of General Practitioners, London.

215. Illingworth, R. S. (1987). Pitfalls in developmental diagnosis. *Archives of Disease in Childhood* **62**, 860–5.

216. Roberts, C. J. and Khosla, T. (1972). An evaluation of developmental examination as a method of detecting neurological, visual and auditory handicaps in infancy. *British Journal of Preventive and Social Medicine* **26**, 94–100.

217. Ellenberg, J. B. and Nelson, K. B. (1981). Early recognition of infants at high risk of cerebral palsy. *Developmental Medicine and Child Neurology* **23**, 705–16.

218. Wells, C. G. (1986). Variation in child language. In *Language acquisition* (ed. P. Fletcher and M. Carman), 2nd edn. Cambridge University Press, Cambridge.

219. Silva, P. A. (1987). Epidemiology, longitudinal course, and some associated factors: an update. In *Language development and disorders* (ed. W. Yule and M. Rutter), pp. 1–15. Clinics in Developmental Medicine No. 101/102. Mackeith Press/Blackwell, Oxford.

220. Bishop, D. V. M. and Edmundson, A. (1987). Language-impaired 4-year-olds; distinguishing transient from persistent impairment. *Journal of Speech and Hearing Disorders* **52**, 156–73.

221. Bishop, D. V. M. and Edmundson, A. (1987). Specific language impairment as a maturational lag; evidence from longitudinal data on language and motor development. *Developmental Medicine and Child Neurology* **29**, 442–59.

222. Martin, J. A. M. (1981). Voice, speech and language in the child; development and disorder. *Disorders of human communication*, Vol. 4. Springer-Verlag, Wien.

223. Henderson, S. E. (1987). The assessment of 'clumsy' children; old and new approaches. *Journal of Child Psychology and Psychiatry* **28**, 511–28.

224. Robson, P. (1970). Shuffling, hitching, scooting or sliding, observations in 30 otherwise normal children. *Developmental Medicine and Child Neurology* 12, 608–17.

225. Haidvogl, M. (1979). Dissociation of Maturation. A distinct syndrome of delayed motor development. *Developmental Medicine and Child Neurology* 21, 52–7.

226. Newson, E. (1976). Parents as a resource in diagnosis and assessment. Early management of handicapping disorders. IRMMH *Review of Research and Practice* 19, 105–17.

227. Cooper, N. A. and Lynch, M. A. (1979). Lost to follow-up. A study of non-attendance. *Archives of Disease in Childhood* 54, 765–9.

228. Bicknell, J. (1983). The psychopathology of handicap. *British Journal of Medical Psychology* 56, 167–78.

229. Kew, S. (1975). *Handicap and family crisis.* Invalid Children's Aid Association/Pitman, London.

230. Bradley, R. H. (1986). Assessing the family environment of young children. In *Theory and research in behavioural pediatrics* (ed. H. E. Fitzgerald, B. M. Lester, and M. W. Yogman), pp. 47–97. Plenum Press, New York and London.

231. Purser, H. (1987). Special Education. In *Language development and disorders* (ed. W. Yule and M. Rutter), pp. 436–48. Clinics in Developmental Medicine No. 101/102. Mackeith Press/Blackwell, Oxford.

232. Bishop, D. V. M. (1987). The concept of comprehension in language disorder. In *Proceedings of the first international symposium on specific speech and language disorders in children*, pp. 75–87. Association for All Speech Impaired Children (AFASIC), London*.

233. Gordon, N. (1987). Developmental disorders of speech and language. In *Language development and disorders* (ed. W. Yule and M. Rutter), pp. 189–205. Clinics in Developmental Medicine No. 101/102. Mackeith Press/Blackwell, Oxford.

234. Rapin, I. (1987). Developmental dysphasia and autism in pre-school children; characteristics and subtypes. In *Proceedings of the first international symposium on specific speech and language disorders in children*, pp. 20–35. Association for All Speech Impaired Children (AFASIC), London*.

235. Miller, J. F. (1987). A grammatical characterization of language disorder. In *Proceedings of the first international symposium on specific speech and language disorders in children*, pp. 100–13. Association for All Speech Impaired Children (AFASIC), London.*

* Available from: AFASIC, 347 Central Markets, Smithfield, London EC1.

236. Berger, M. (1987). What is a language disorder? In *Proceedings of the first international symposium on specific speech and language disorders in children*, pp. 61–74. Association for All Speech Impaired Children (AFASIC), London*.

237. Bishop, D. V. M. (1987). The causes of specific developmental language disorder ('developmental dysphasia'). *Journal of Child Psychology and Psychiatry and Allied Disciplines* **28**, 1–8.

238. Crystal, D. (1981). *Clinical linguistics. Disorders of human communication.* Springer, Berlin.

239. Cromer, R. F. (1981). *Early language, acquisition and intervention* (ed. R. L. Schiefelbusch and D. D. Bricker). Language intervention series, Vol. 6. University Park Press, Baltimore.

240. Snyder-McLean, L. and McLean, J. E. (1987). Effectiveness of early intervention for children with language and communication disorders. In *The effectiveness of early intervention for at-risk and handicapped chldren* (ed. M. J. Guralnick and F. C. Bennett), pp. 213–74. Academic Press, Orlando, Florida and London.

241. Bernstein, B. (1970). Education cannot compensate for society. *New Society* **387**, 344–7.

242. Clarke, A. M. and Clarke, A. D. B. (1976). *Early experience: myth and evidence.* Open Books, London and Free Press, New York.

243. Cunningham, C. (1974). Training and education approaches for parents of children with special needs. *British Journal of Medical Psychology* **58**, 285–305.

244. Rutter, M. (1980). The long-term effects of early experience. *Developmental Medicine and Child Neurology* **22**, 800–15.

245. Clarke, A. M. and Clarke, A. D. B. (1986). Thirty years of child psychology: a selective review. *Journal of Child Psychology and Psychiatry* **27**, 719–60.

246. Connolly, K. (1972). Learning and the concept of critical periods in infancy. *Developmental Medicine and Child Neurology* **14**, 705–14.

247. Skuse, D. (1984). Extreme deprivation in early childhood. II Theoretical issues and a comparative review. *Journal of Child Psychology and Psychiatry* **25**, 543–72.

248. Evans, E. D. (1982). Longitudinal follow-up assessment of differential preschool experience for low income minority group children. *Journal of Educational Research* **78**, 197–202.

249. Lazar, I. and Darlington, R. B. (1982). Lasting effects of early education. *Monographs of the Society for Research in Child Development* **47**, 1–151.

250. Woodhead, M. (1985). Pre-school education has long-term effects: but can they be generalised? *Oxford Review of Education* **11**, 133–55.

251. Rathbone, M. and Graham, N. C. (1981). Parent participation in the primary school. *Education Studies* **7**, 145–50.

252. Clark, M. M. and Cheyne, W. M. (1979). *Studies in pre-school education*. Scottish Council for Research in Education. Hodder & Stoughton, Sevenoaks.

253. Tizard B. *et al.* (1983). Language and Social Class; is verbal deprivation a myth? *Journal of Child Psychology and Psychiatry* **24**, 533–42.

254. Palfrey, J. S., Walker, D. K., Sullivan, M., and Levine, M. D. (1987). Targeted early childhood programming; the promise half-fulfilled. *American Journal of Diseases of Children* **141**, 55–9.

255. Pearson, L. and Lindsay, G. (1986). *Special needs in the primary school*. NFER/Nelson, Windsor.

256. Whitmore, T. K. (1987). Screening in child health. *Proceedings of the Royal College of Physicians* (Edinburgh) **17**, 25–36.

257. Whitmore, K. (1985). *Health services in schools—a new look*. Spastics International Medical Publications.

258. Leach, D. J. (1981). *Screening for school learning difficulties*. Occasional papers of the British Psychological Society; Division of Educational and Child Psychology, Vol. 5 Part 2, pp. 46–59. London.

259. Wedell, K. and Lindsay, G. A. (1980). Early identification procedures; what have we learned? *Remedial Education* **15**, 130–5.

260. Bax, M. and Whitmore, K. (1987). The medical examination of children on entry to school. The results and use of neurodevelopmental assessment. *Developmental Medicine and Child Neurology* **29**, 40–55.

261. Whitmore, K. and Bax, M. (1986). The school entrant medical examination. *Archives of Disease in Childhood* **61**, 807–17.

262. Tizard, J., Schofield, W. N., and Hewison, J. (1982). Collaboration between teachers and parents in assisting children's reading. *British Journal of Educational Psychology* **52**, 1–15.

263. Harrison, M. and Hart, L. (1987). "Home-start". In *Progress in Child Health* (ed. J. A. Macfarlane), Vol. 3. Churchill Livingstone, Edinburgh.

264. Rathbone, M. and Graham, N. C. (1981). Parent participation in the primary school. *Educational Studies*, **7**, 145–50. Berks.

265. Mortimore, P., Sammons, P., Stoll, L., Lewis, D., and Ecob, R. (1988). *School matters; the junior years*. Open Books, Wells, Somerset.

266. Newby, M. and Nicoll, A. (1985). Selection of children for school medicals by a pastoral care system in an inner-city junior school. *Public Health* (London) **99**, 331–7.

267. O'Callaghan, E. M. and Colver, A. F. (1987). Selective medical examination on starting school. *Archives of Disease in Childhood* **62**, 1041–3.

268. Earls, F. (1980). Prevalence of behaviour problems in three-year-old children. A cross-national replication. *Archives of General Psychiatry* **37**, 1153–7.

269. Richman, N., Stevenson, J., and Graham, P. (1977). Prevalence of behaviour problems in pre-school children: an epidemiological study in a London borough. *Journal of Child Psychology and Psychiatry* **16**, 277–87.

270. Richman, N., Stevenson, J., and Graham, P. (1982). *Pre-school to school: a behavioural study.* Academic Press, London.

271. Graham, P. (1986). Pre-school behavioural adjustment disorders. In *Child psychiatry. A developmental approach* (ed. P. J. Graham), pp. 80–3. Oxford University Press, Oxford.

272. Richman, H. (1985). Disorders in pre-school children. In *Child and adolescent Psychiatry* (ed. M. Rutter and L. Hersov), pp. 336–50. Blackwell, Oxford.

273. Richman, N. and Graham, P. (1971). A behaviour screening questionnaire for use with pre-school children. *Journal of Child Psychology and Psychiatry* **12**, 5–33.

274. Hill, P. (1982). Behaviour modification with children. *British Journal of Hospital Medicine* **27**, 51–60.

275. Richman, N. (1985). Sleep disorders in young children. In *Progress in Child Health* (ed. J. A. Macfarlane), Vol. 2. Churchill Livingstone, Edinburgh.

276. Richman, N. (1977). Is a behaviour check-list for pre-school children useful? In *Epidemiological approaches in child psychiatry* (ed. P. J. Graham), pp. 125–37. Academic Press, London.

277. Shadish, W. R. (1982). A review and critique of controlled studies of the effectiveness of preventive child health care. *Health Policy Quarterly* **2**, 52.

278. Dworkin, P. H. *et al.* (1987). Does developmental content influence the effectiveness of anticipatory guidance? *Pediatrics* **80**, 196–202.

279. Cadman, D. *et al.* (1987). Evaluation of public health preschool child developmental screening; the process and outcomes of a community program. *American Journal of Public Health* **77**, 45–51.

280. Dershewitz, R. A. and Williamson, J. W. (1977). Prevention of childhood household injuries: a controlled clinical trial. *American Journal of Public Health* **67**, 1148–53.

281. Robertson, L. S. (1987). *Childhood injuries: knowledge and strategies for prevention.* Prepared for the Office of Technology Assessment, US Congress, Washington.

282. Reisinger, K. S. *et al.* (1981). Effects of pediatricians' counselling on infant restraint use. *Pediatrics* **67**, 201–6.

283. US Department of Health and Human Services, Public Health Service, Centers for Disease Control (1983). Premature mortality due to unintentional injuries—United States. *Morbidity and Mortality Weekly Report* **35**, 353–6.

284. Dietz, P. E. and Baker, S. P. (1974). Drowning; epidemiology and prevention. *American Journal of Public Health* **64**, 303–12.

285. Baker, S. P. (1981). Childhood injuries: the community approach to prevention. *Public Health Policy* **2**, 235–46.

286. Jackson, R. H., Cooper, S., and Hayes, H. R. M. (1988). The work of the child accident prevention trust. *Archives of Disease in Childhood* **63**, 318–20.

287. Gallagher, S. S., Hunter, P., and Guyer, B. (1985). A home injury prevention program for children. *Pediatric Clinics of North America* **32**, 95–112.

288. Bass, J. L. *et al.* (1985). Educating parents about injury prevention. *Pediatric Clinics of North America* **32**, 233–41.

289. Miller, R. E., *et al.* (1982). Pediatric counselling and subsequent use of smoke detectors. *American Journal of Public Health* **72**, 392–3.

290. Haddon, W., Jr (1980). Advances in the epidemiology of injuries as a basis for public policy. *Public Health Reports* **95**, 411.

291. Casey, P. H. and Whitt, J. K. (1980). Effect of the pediatrician on the mother—infant relationship. *Pediatrics* **65**, 815–20.

292. Casey, P. H. *et al.* Developmental intervention: a pediatric clinical review. *Pediatric Clinics of North America* **33**, 899–923.

293. Resnick, M. B. *et al.* (1987). Developmental intervention for low birth weight infants; improved early development outcome. *Pediatrics* **80**, 68–74.

294. Williams, A. F. (1987). Recent advances in infant feeding. In *Progress in Child Health* (ed. J. A. Macfarlane), Vol. 3. Churchill Livingstone, Edinburgh.

295. Cullen, K. J. (1976). A six-year controlled trial of prevention of children's behavior disorders. *Pediatrics* **88**, 662–6.

296. Gutelius, M. F. *et al.* (1977). Controlled study of child health supervision; behavioral results. *Pediatrics* **60**, 294–304.

297. Jenner, A. M. and Lennon, M. A. (1986). An evaluation of the school dental inspections. *Community Dental Health* **3**, 221–6.

298. Todd, J. E. and Dodd, T. (1985). *Children's dental health in the United Kingdom.* HMSO, London.

299. Sheiham, A. (1986). Public dental health perspectives. *Radical Community Medicine,* Autumn, 34–7.

300. Bradshaw, W. C. L. (1985). Dental problems in children. In *Progress in Child Health* (ed. J. A. Macfarlane), Vol. 2. Churchill Livingstone, Edinburgh.

301. Seagull, E. A. W. (1987). Social support and child maltreatment: a review of the evidence. *Child Abuse and Neglect* 11, 41–52.

302. Straus, M. A. (1980). Stress and child abuse. In *The battered child* (ed. C. H. Kempe and R. E. Helfer). University of Chicago Press, Chicago.

303. Smith, S. M., Hanson, R., and Noble, S. (1973). Parents of battered babies. A controlled study. *British Medical Journal* 4, 388–91.

304. Siegel, E. *et al.* (1980). Hospital and home support during infancy: impact on maternal attachment, child abuse and neglect, and health care utilization. *Pediatrics* 66, 183–90.

305. Steinberg, L. D., Catalano, R., and Dooley, D. (1981). Economic antecedents of child abuse and neglect. *Child Development* 52, 975–85.

306. Finkelhor, C. and Araji, S. (1986). *A source book on child sexual abuse.* Sage Publications, Beverly Hills.

307. Olds, D. L. and Henderson, C. R. (1988). The prevention of maltreatment. In *Child maltreatment; research and theory on the consequences of child abuse and neglect* (ed. D. Cicchetti and V. Carlson). Cambridge University Press, Cambridge.

308. Olds, D. L. *et al.* (1986). Preventing child abuse and neglect: a randomized trial of nurse home visitation. *Pediatrics* 78, 65–78.

309. Lally, J. R. (1984). Three views of child neglect; expanding visions of preventive intervention. *Child Abuse and Neglect* 8, 243–5.

310. Taylor, B., Wadsworth, J., and Butler, N. R. (1983). Teenage mothering, admission to hospital and accidents during the first 5 years. *Archives of Disease in Childhood* 58, 6–11.

311. Macfarlane, A., McPherson, A., McPherson, K., and Ahmed, L. (1987). Teenagers and their health. *Archives of Disease in Childhood* 62, 1125–9.

312. Watson, J. M. (1985). Glue sniffing. In *Progress in Child Health* (ed. J. A. Macfarlane), Vol. 2. Churchill Livingstone, Edinburgh.

313. Vlies, R. (1985). Gynaecological problems of adolescents. In *Progress in Child Health* (ed. J. A. Macfarlane), Vol. 2. Churchill Livingstone, Edinburgh.

314. O'Flaherty, S., Jandera, E., Llewellyn, J., and Wall, M. (1987). Personal health records; an evaluation. *Archives of Disease in Childhood* **62**, 1152–5.

315. Rigby, M. J. (1987). The national child health computer system. In *Progress in Child Health* (ed. J. A. Macfarlane), Vol. 3. Churchill Livingstone, Edinburgh.

316. Edwards, B. (1987). Child health records and the computer. In *Progress in Child Health* (ed. J. A. Macfarlane), Vol. 3. Churchill Livingstone, Edinburgh.

317. Waterston, T. (1987). Medical education in child health. In *Progress in Child Health* (ed. J. A. Macfarlane), Vol. 3. Churchill Livingstone, Edinburgh.

318. Quinton, D. (1988). Urbanism and mental health. *Journal of Child Psychology and Psychiatry* **29**, 11–20.

319. Roche, S. and Stacey, M. (1984). Overview of research on the provision and utilization of child health services. Department of Health and Social Security, London.

320. Roche, S. and Stacey, M. (1986). Overview of research on the provision and utilization of child health services; update I. Department of Health and Social Security, London.

321. Roche, S. and Stacey, M. (1987). Overview of research on the provision and utilization of child health services; update II. Department of Health and Social Security, London.

322. Sefi, S. and Macfarlane, A. (1985). Why mothers attend Child Health Clinics. *Health Visitor* **58**, 129–30.

323. Sel, J. (1982). Will you weigh my baby, lady? *Nursing Times* 1620–4.

324. Watson, E. (1986). A mis-match of goals? *Health Visitor* **59**, 75–9.

325. Nicoll, A., Mann, S., Mann, N., and Vyas, H. (1986). The child health clinic; results of a new strategy of community care in a deprived area. *Lancet* 15 March, 606–8.

326. Curtis-Jenkins, G. H. (1987). Child health in general practice. In *Progress in Child Health* (ed. J. A. Macfarlane), Vol. 3. Churchill Livingstone, Edinburgh.

327. Polnay, L. (1984). The community paediatric team—an approach to child health services in a deprived inner city area. In *Progress in Child Health* (ed. J. A. Macfarlane), Vol. 1. Churchill Livingstone, Edinburgh.

328. Hart, H., Bax, M., and Jenkins, S. (1981). Use of the child health clinic. *Archives of Disease in Childhood* **56**, 440–5.

329. Dworkin, P. H. *et al.* (1979). Training in developmental pediatrics; how practitioners perceive the gap. *American Journal of Diseases of Children* **133**, 709–12.
330. Bennett, F. C. *et al.* (1984). Teaching developmental pediatrics to pediatric residents; effectiveness of a structured curriculum. *Pediatrics* **74**, 514–22.

Appendix 1

Format for initial report on individual screening procedures

1. Definition of each disease/disorder/problem.
2. Incidence (where known)—from whole population studies, such as cohort studies. Also give incidence on sub-populations where appropriate.
3. Natural history including outcomes with and without intervention.
4. What treatment/intervention is available.
5. List the arguments for and against screening.
6. If a screening programme is thought to be justified, at what age(s) should it be carried out.
7. Is there a primary screening test in common use for the whole population? Are there secondary screening tests before final diagnosis. (NB Screening tests are to identify a high risk population from a low risk population and may simply be asking a question like 'did the child have fits at birth').
8. What are the tests—describe briefly.
9. Performance characteristics (where known):
    (a) validity;
    (b) false + / − rates;
    (c) cost (materials and time taken to do the test);
    (d) acceptability to the public/patient.
10. Research studies undertaken on whole populations or sub-populations.
11. Referral implications for specialist services, i.e. how many referrals are generated by the screening process.
12. How the success of the screening programme can be monitored from a service point of view.
13. Suggest any future research needs to validate screening programmes.
14. Bibliography—list summary and review articles separately. Please attach front page of main articles if possible.
15. List people consulted where appropriate.

Appendix 2

The working party thank the following individuals and organizations who were invited to submit comments and suggestions:

Ms Mary Holland
Secretary, Medical Advisory Panel
MENCAP
123 Golden Lane
London
EC1Y 0RT

Mr Ian Bruce
Director-General
RNIB
224 Great Portland Street
London
W1N 6AA

Mr H. Piggett
President, Scoliosis Society
7 Chard Road
Edgbaston
Birmingham
B15 3EN

Ms L. Watling
Education Officer
National Deaf Children's Society
45 Hereford Road
London
W2 5AH

Mrs B. McAlpine
Spastic Society Assessment Centre
16 Fitzroy Square
London
W1P 6HQ

Mrs S. D. Rudder
Sickle Cell Society
Green Lodge
Barretts Green Road
London
NW10 7AP

Ms Norma Corkish
Director
AFASIC
347 Central Market
London
EC1A 9NH

Ms Philippa Russell
Voluntary Council for
    Handicapped Children
8 Wakley Street
London
EC1V 7QE

Mr Tam Fry
Chairman, Child Growth
    Foundation
2 Mayfield Avenue
London
W4 1PW

Mr R. Clark
Director, SENSE
311 Grays Inn Road
London
WC1X 8PT

Lady Lovell-Davis
NAWCH
Argyle House
29–31 Euston Road
London
NW1 2SD

Ms Usha Prashar
National Council for Voluntary
  Organisations
26 Bedford Square
London
WC1B 3HU

Ms Hannah Corbishley
National Childbirth Trust
9 Queensborough Terrace
London
W2 3TB

Mrs J. Digby
Information Officer
Pre-School Playgroups
  Association
61 Kings Cross Road
London
WC1X 9LL

Dr Heather Kilgore
Dept Health & Social Services
Dundonald House
Upper Newtownards Road
Belfast
BT4 3SF

Dr D. Ferguson-Lewis
Crown Offices
Cathays Park
Cardiff
CF1 3NQ

Countess of Limerick
Foundation for the Study of
  Infant Deaths
15 Belgrave Square
London
SW1X 8PS

Mr David Hart (NAHT)
Holly House
6 Paddockhall Road
Haywards Heath
W Sussex
RH16 1RG

Ms E. Darbyshire
Health & Safety Dept
National Union of Teachers
Hamilton House
Mabledon Place
London
WC1H 9BD

Ms Marianne Rigge
College of Health
14 Buckingham Street
London
WC2N 6DS

Mrs G. Dishart
Dept of Education & Science
Elizabeth House
York Road
London
SE1 7PH

Mr R. Davie
National Children's Bureau
8 Wakley Street
London
EC1V 7QE

Professor B. McKibbin
President
British Orthopaedic Association
35 Lincoln's Inn Fields
London
WC2A 3PN

Mr Barrie Jay
President, Faculty of
  Opthalmologists
Moorfields Eye Hospital
City Road
London
EC1V 2PD

Dr Barry McCormick
Audiological Scientist
Children's Hearing Assessment
  Centre
General Hospital
Nottingham
NG1 6FY

Mr Charles Smith
President, British Assocn of
  Otolaryngologists
35 Lincoln's Inn Fields
London
WC2A 3PN

Dr R. O. Robinson
Convener, British Paediatric
  Neurology Association
Guy's Hospital
St Thomas's Street
London
SE1 9RT

Mr D. Wiseman
Administrator
College of Speech Therapists
6 Lechmere Road
London
NW2 5BU

Dr Rosemary Rue
Faculty of Community Medicine
4 St Andrew's Place
London
NW1 4LB

Mr G. J. B. Claredge
Secretary
College of Occupational
  Therapists
20 Rede Place
London
W2 4TU

Mr T. Simon
Secretary
Chartered Society of
  Physiotherapy
14 Bedford Row
London
WC1R 4ED

Mrs J. Batchelor
General Secretary
Scottish Health Visitors
  Association
94 Constitution Street
Edinburgh
EH6 6AW

Ms Ruth Ashton
Royal College of Midwives
15 Mansfield Street
London
W1M 0BE

Ms Elspeth Brewis
Assn of British Paediatric Nurses
Dept of Child Health
Royal Hospital for Sick Children
Yorkhill
Glasgow
G3 8SJ

Mrs M. Dams
Chairman, ASNA
8 Western Road
Henley on Thames
Oxon
RG14 1JL

Dr J. O. Warner
The Brompton Hospital
Fulham Road
London
SW3 6HP

Dr E. A. Shinebourne
The Brompton Hospital
Fulham Road
London
SW3 6HP

Professor K. Wedell
Institute of Education
20 Bedford Way
London
WC1H 0AL

Ms Clair Chilvers
Institute of Cancer Research
Clifton Avenue
Sutton
Surrey
SM2 5PX

Professor P. J. Graham
Dept of Child Psychiatry
Hospital for Sick Children
Great Ormond Street
London
WC1N 3JH

Professor K. S. Holt
The Wolfson Centre
Mecklenburgh Square
London
WC1N 2AP

Dr L. Polnay
Floor E, East Block
University Hospital
Queens Medical Centre
Nottingham
NG7 2UH

Dr A. F. Colver
Beaconhill Children's Centre
163 Langdale Drive
Cramlington
Northumberland
NE23 8EH

Professor J. Butler
Health Services Research Unit
University of Kent
Canterbury
Kent
CT2 7NF

Dr Margaret Pollack
Sheldon Children's Centre
Kings College Hospital
Denmark Hill
London
SE5 8RX

Professor D. J. Weatherall
Nuffield Dept of Clinical
    Medicine
John Radcliffe Hospital
Headington
Oxford
OX3 9DU

Professor C. Chantler
Evelina Children's Hospital
Guy's Hospital
St Thomas Street
London
SE1 9RT

Dr M. de Swiet
Queen Charlotte's Maternity
  Hospital
Goldhawk Road
London
W6 0XG

Dr Doreen Roberts
British Association of Doctors
  in Audiology
3 Linden Road
Manchester
M20 8QJ

Mr L. Lightman
Honorary Secretary
British Orthoptic Society
Tavistock House
Tavistock Square
London
WC1H 9JP

Miss Pauline Smith
Chairman
British Association of
  Audiological Scientists
General Hospital
Nottingham
NG1 6HA

Professor R. Hinchcliffe
Chairman, British Association
  of Audiological Physicians
Audiological Centre
National Throat & Ear Hospital
Grays Inn Road
London WC1

Dr Philip Hunt
Director, NAHA
Garth House
47 Edgbaston Park Road
Birmingham
B15 2RS

Dr S. L. Stewart-Brown
Dept of Community Medicine
Southmead Hospital
Westbury on Trym
Bristol
BS10 5NB

Dr Martin Bellman
Nuffield Centre
National Throat & Ear Hospital
Grays Inn Road
London WC1

Professor J. K. Lloyd
Institute of Child Health
30 Guilford Street
London WC1

Professor M. A. Preece
Institute of Child Health
30 Guilford Street
London WC1

Dr Sue Jenkins
Dept of Community Medicine
St Leonards Hospital
London N1

Index